Major Power Relations in Northeast Asia

The Asia Society is a nonprofit, nonpartisan public education organization dedicated to increasing American understanding of Asia and its growing importance to the United States and to world relations. Founded in 1956, the Society covers all of Asia—22 countries from Japan to Iran and from Soviet Central Asia to the South Pacific islands. Through its programs in contemporary affairs, the fine and performing arts, and elementary and secondary education, the Society reaches audiences across the United States and works closely with colleagues in Asia.

The *Asian Agenda* program of The Asia Society seeks to . . .

- Alert Americans to the key Asian issues of the 1980s
- Illuminate the policy choices facing decision-makers in the public and private sectors
- Strengthen the dialogue between Americans and Asians on the issues and their policy implications.

Asian Agenda issues are identified in consultation with a group of advisors and are addressed through studies and publications, national and international conferences, public programs around the U.S., and media activities. Major funding for the Asian Agenda program is currently provided by the Ford Foundation, the Rockefeller Foundation, the Andrew W. Mellon Foundation, the Henry Luce Foundation, the Rockefeller Brothers Fund, and the United States-Japan Foundation.

MAJOR POWER RELATIONS IN NORTHEAST ASIA

by Robert A. Scalapino

THE ASIA SOCIETY

UNIVERSITY PRESS OF AMERICA

LANHAM • NEW YORK • LONDON

Copyright © 1987 by

University Press of America,® Inc.

4720 Boston Way
Lanham, MD 20706

3 Henrietta Street
London WC2E 8LU England

British Cataloging in Publication Information Available

Co-published by arrangement with
The Asia Society,
725 Park Avenue, New York, New York 10021

Library of Congress Cataloging in Publication Data

Scalapino, Robert A.
  Major power relations in Northeast Asia.

  (Asian agenda report ; 9)
  1. East Asia—Foreign relations.   I. Title.
II. Series.
DS518.1.S32   1986   327.5   86-22442
ISBN 0-8191-5679-5 (alk. paper)
ISBN 0-8191-5680-9 (pbk. : alk. paper)

Contents

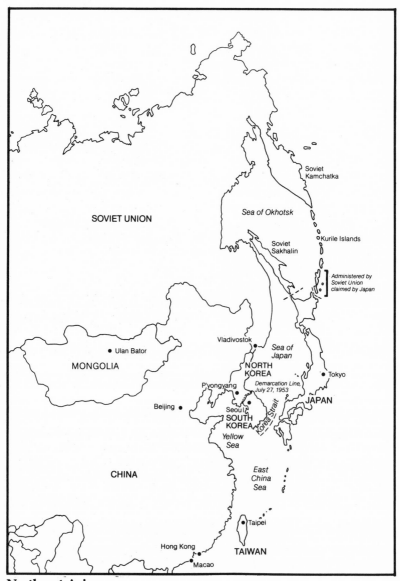

Northeast Asia

Foreword

In the years ahead Japan and the United States will face challenges to their interests and to their partnership in the Asian regional setting. How the two nations respond to changing conditions in the region will have significant consequences for other nations as well. The challenge is especially evident in Northeast Asia, where vital security interests of both nations are at stake and where economic relations are changing rapidly.

The Soviet military buildup in Northeast Asia, the confrontations on the Korean peninsula, the evolution of the Sino-Soviet relationship, and the Taiwan question make the security situation in the region one of the most sensitive and complex in the world. Political and security relations are further complicated by historic economic developments such as the opening and reform of China's economy, the emergence of Korea and Taiwan as major trading nations and competitors with Japan in some sectors, and the mounting pressure on Japan to reorient its economy. While most Americans and Japanese are focusing their attention on strains in their bilateral relationship, the potential for cooperation and conflict arising from these trends and issues has received relatively little notice. But successful management of U.S.-Japan interactions in Northeast Asia will require wider understanding in both countries.

This report is one result of a multiyear project sponsored by The Asia Society that seeks to stimulate greater American attention to U.S.-Japan interactions in Asia. The first phase of the project on "Japan, the United States and a Changing Asia" focused on Japanese and American interests and roles in Southeast Asia. It included an international conference in Japan in July 1984 that brought together more than fifty Americans, Japanese and Southeast Asians, a report authored by Charles Morrison of the East-West Center and published in the Asian Agenda report series, and a series of regional programs held in seven U.S. cities in February 1985.

The second phase of the project has examined the multilateral relations of Japan and the United States in Northeast Asia and has sought to stimulate wider discussion of them between Americans and Japanese and in the United States. In the fall of 1985 The Asia Society organized two study missions. The first, consisting of seven American specialists on Asian affairs, visited seven political and financial capitals of Northeast Asia to obtain the views of government officials, scholars, business people, educators and journalists on the international relations of the region. A second study team consisting of fifteen leaders from across the United States drawn from several professional fields visited Japan for a week of briefings and discusssions with Japanese officials, scholars and journalists on Northeast Asian affairs. A conference in Japan in November 1985 brought the two American teams together with Japanese counterparts for an exchange of views on the region.

This process of international dialogue provided the basis for an array of education outreach activities in the United States. These included lectures by the American specialists in different parts of the United States during the winter and spring of 1986, miniconferences in six American cities during May 1986 in which the American specialists and visiting Asian scholars discussed the region before diverse audiences, and a series of monographs by the American specialists on key topics relating to Japan and the United States in Northeast Asia. These monographs, including the present volume, are being published separately by The Asia Society in its Asian Agenda report series for wide distribution around the United States and Asia.

The specialist study mission was led by Professor Robert A. Scalapino of the University of California at Berkeley, one of the United States' leading authorities on Asian affairs. The other members included distinguished scholars representing different disciplines and area specialties: Herbert Ellison, an historian of Russia and the Soviet Union who was then director of the Kennan Institute of Advanced Russian Studies in Washington, D.C. and is now at the University of Washington, Seattle; Harry Harding, a political scientist specializing on China and Senior Fellow at the Brookings Institution; Donald Hellmann, a scholar of Japanese politics and foreign policy at the University of Washington, Seattle; Nicholas Lardy, a specialist on the Chinese economy also at the University of Washington, Seattle; Edward J. Lincoln, an economist working on Japan at the Brookings Institution; and myself (Marshall M. Bouton), representing The Asia Society.

Over a period of five weeks in October-November 1985 the Northeast Asian study mission visited Tokyo, Moscow, Ulan Bator, Beijing, Hong Kong, Taipei and Seoul. The mission also sought to visit Pyongyang but was not granted permission to do so by the North Korean authorities. In the course of its mission the American team met with over two hundred and fifty officials, scholars, journalists and business people. This intensive schedule of discussions was made possible through the generous assistance of host organizations in all seven cities: the Japan Center for International Exchange in Tokyo; the Institute of Oriental Studies in Moscow; the Executive Committee of the Union of Mongolian Organizations for Peace and Friendship with Other Countries in Ulan Bator; the Chinese Academy of Social Sciences in Beijing; the Universities Service Center in Hong Kong; the Institute of International Relations in Taipei; and the Asiatic Research Center of Korea University in Seoul. The Asia Society is deeply grateful for this assistance.

This report is the latest in a series produced by The Asia Society's national public education program on contemporary Asian affairs, "America's Asian Agenda". The Asian Agenda program seeks to alert Americans to critical issues in Asian affairs and in U.S.-Asia relations, to illuminate the choices which public and private policy-makers face, and to strengthen trans-Pacific dialogue on the issues. Through studies, national and international conferences, regional public programs in the United States, and corporate and media activities, the program involves American and Asian specialists and opinion-leaders in a far-reaching educational process. Asian Agenda publications emphasize short, timely reports aimed at a wide readership. Other recently published and forthcoming Asian Agenda reports address a variety of topics including Christianity in contemporary Korea, the United States and the ANZUS alliance, financing Asian growth and development, and the Philippines and the United States.

The Asia Society wishes to acknowledge the roles played by a number of individuals and organizations in the activities leading to this report. First, the Society is deeply indebted to Robert A. Scalapino for his extraordinary leadership of the American specialist mission to Northeast Asia. His exceptional knowledge, energy and goodwill were essential to the success of a complex and demanding endeavor. The Society is equally grateful to the other distinguished team members for their valuable contributions to the mission and other components of the project. Special thanks are also due to the leaders of the Asian organizations that arranged our programs: Tadashi Yamamoto, Evgenii Primakov, Luvsanchultem, Zhao Fusan, John Dolfin, Yu-Ming Shaw and Han Sung-Joo. We wish also to express deep appreciation to the many individuals in the cities visited who took time from their very busy schedules to talk with the team at length.

Major financial support for the project on "Japan, the United States and a Changing Northeast Asia" has been generously provided by the United States-Japan Foundation. The Japan-United States Friendship Commission made available monies for the U.S. regional programming of the project. Critical also was funding provided for the Society's Asian Agenda program by the Ford, Rockefeller and Henry Luce foundations and the Rockefeller Brothers Fund.

Finally, several members of the Society's staff were instrumental in the development of the project and the publications. John Bresnan assisted in the project's original overall design. Ernest Notar played an important early role in the project's phase on Northeast Asia. Most

ix

central to that second phase were Timothy J.C. O'Shea, who very ably organized all the project's activities, and Rose Wright, who provided excellent administrative assistance. Eileen D. Chang skillfully guided the publication of this and other reports emerging from the project.

Marshall M. Bouton
Director, Contemporary Affairs
The Asia Society
June, 1986

Preface

If one had to choose a single region of greatest importance to Americans in terms of their livelihood, political values and security, a leading candidate would be Northeast Asia. It is here that the most intensive economic interaction involving the United States will take place in the years immediately ahead, with interdependence—and the problems attendant to it—steadily advancing. It is here that the capacities of diverse societies to achieve and maintain a greater degree of political openness will be tested. And it is here that global and regional security issues are inextricably connected, with fateful consequences for all mankind.

In considering the future of Northeast Asia, one must juxtapose two equally important factors. On the one hand, each of the nation-states within the region bears a primary responsibility for the welfare of its own people, and the strength of its domestic political and social fabric. The decisions made by the leaders of each society are especially crucial at a time when virtually every government stands at a crossroads, facing the necessity of reconsidering past economic policies, political institutions and security strategies. Any attempt to shift the principal responsibility to external forces is fallacious.

At the same time, two nations—the United States and Japan—are deeply interrelated with both the developmental and security issues that confront the region as a whole. In their very dynamism, and the extraordinary reach of their power—economic, political or military - they cannot avoid exerting a major influence throughout Northeast Asia. Inaction as well as action sends its message, creates an impact. Their domestic policies no less than their foreign policies have far-reaching repercussions.

It thus seemed important and timely to undertake a study on United States and Japanese policies in a changing Northeast Asia. In liaison with knowledgeable Japanese, we set about examining our respective roles in the region—past, present and future.

Our task was to draw upon our background as students of Asia, supplementing this with a journey to all parts of the region available to us to hear the current ideas and proposals of Asians representing various political, economic and national perspectives. During the course of our five-week trip, we sought first to discern those indigenous elements of a geopolitical, ideological or economic nature that helped to shape a given society's attitudes and policies toward its neighbors, toward the region as a whole and especially toward the United States and Japan. We also explored the issues of greatest concern to our respondents and their views as to the appropriate remedial action. At various points, attention focused upon the question of American and Japanese policies, with an effort to examine viable alternatives as well as the potentials that existed in current policies.

On occasion, as individuals we held different views from our Asian or Soviet friends, either with respect to the relevant data or the conclusions to be drawn from it. Being Americans, moreover, we sometimes differed among ourselves. The monograph that follows, and the others in this series, thus represent the views of the author. No effort has been made to achieve a complete consensus among us. Nevertheless, those who read all of the monographs will discover a very considerable measure of agreement on most matters of consequence.

We are enormously grateful to those individuals and organizations throughout Northeast Asia and in the Soviet Union who served as hosts, facilitators and discussants. To exchange views in a concentrated fashion, and to have the opportunity to compare and contrast the views in one society with those in another over a very short period of time proved both enlightening and stimulating.

On behalf of the group, let me also express our deep gratitude to The Asia Society and its principal officers, especially Marshall Bouton, for making possible an experience that was both enriching and enjoyable.

Robert A. Scalapino
Berkeley, California

Executive Summary

Today, Northeast Asia is at the vortex of that vast area that we call Pacific Asia, a part of the globe destined to shape the twenty-first century economically, politically and strategically. Economic relations within the region are intense and unbalanced—a volatile combination. Yet few doubt that Northeast Asia together with its major trading partners will set the economic pace for the rest of the world. Politics, however, will remain an independent variable. Together with Japan and China, the United States and the USSR constitute the "big four" of the future, the nations most likely to determine global issues such as war and peace, and, apart from this, to affect the course of organizational efforts beyond the nation-state.

Progress in these directions is made more complex because these states and the broader region of Northeast Asia within which they interact represent the three types of political structure most typical of our age: the democratic, Leninist, and authoritarian-pluralist systems. The two democratic nations, the United States and Japan, operate similar political institutions, though very differently, reflective of the unique cultural antecedents and historical evolution of the two societies. Significant political distinctions appear to be developing between the two large nations flying Leninist banners, the Soviet Union and China. Prediction concerning the diverse authoritarian-pluralist systems is a hazardous task. Broadly speaking, these are societies where a restrictive elitist political structure coexists with and holds power over a pluralist socioeconomic order. South Korea and Taiwan are current examples in Northeast Asia, representing a tiny sample of a system that in its many variations is dominant throughout the so-called Third World.

Beyond the political uncertainties engendered by the competition among these systems, every state of the region is uncomfortably aware of the fact that its own security and that of the two superpowers—the United States and the Soviet Union—cannot easily be separated.

Despite the complexities, a rapid increase of relations between and among the states of this region is taking place. We may define this process as one of Asianization—namely, the intensification of ties between and among the states of the region.

Economic Aspects of Major Power Relations

Four important economic developments can be observed in Northeast Asia. First, in recent years Northeast Asia's economic dynamism has attracted global attention. Second, the societies enjoying the most rapid economic growth have followed the model pioneered by Japan, albeit with suitable variations. Third, a spreading and deepening network of economic ties has been built within Northeast Asia, with Japan as the primary catalyst. This network now transcends ideological-political lines, and represents the single most significant development of the post-1945 decades. Finally, the two economic superpowers, the United States and Japan, have been and will continue to be critical to the course of economic developments within the region.

It is essential, therefore, that both economic superpowers attune their domestic and international economic policies to the changing global environment. The U.S.-Japan relationship, though fundamentally strong, is presently besieged by a variety of economic tensions. Japan's huge trade surplus is as much a source of concern for its trading partners as is the United States' $170 billion (and still growing) trade deficit, half of which can be attributed to the countries of Northeast Asia, particularly Japan. If not properly addressed, America's worsening global economic position can pose serious consequences for the stability of Asian and other economies which rely on U.S. economic strength as a source of their own well being.

Politics and the Major Powers

The political dimensions of major power relations in Northeast Asia rival those in the economic realm in importance and complexity. One major trend of recent decades has been the decline of ideology in virtually all of the major Pacific Asian nations, as leaders increasingly grapple with problems on a pragmatic, experimental basis. Alliances, many of which bound their members together through the common ground of ideology, have similarly been affected, so that today alignments tend to be preferred over alliances. No development is of greater importance to an understanding of international relations at the close of the twentieth century than this trend toward alignments, with all of the fluidity, complexity, and uncertainty that accompanies it. The trend toward alignments as well as the process of Asianization, however, do not necessarily improve the likelihood of an Asian regional structure which many observers have long predicted. Economic and political differences among Asian nations are still strong enough and the influence of the two superpowers pervasive enough to preclude, at least for the forseeable future, a regional structure.

The most important political ties within the region are those between the United States and Japan. Gradually, to be sure, Japan is signaling a more independent diplomacy. This is in line with the general trend away from alliances and towards alignments. If Japan-U.S. political relations are presently strong, Japanese political relations with the Soviet Union are at a low ebb. Polls reveal that the Japanese public has consistently regarded the USSR with the least favor of all foreign nations in recent decades, and more impressionistic evidence indicates that this attitude is reciprocated by Soviet citizens. At best, therefore, the improvement of Soviet-Japanese political relations is likely to be a slow, tortuous process, and dependent in considerable measure upon trends in U.S.-USSR relations.

Meanwhile, Japanese political relations with China have reached a stage which leaders on both sides characterize as "the best in this century." Here, the range of common interests has generally expanded. Yet one should not exaggerate the identity of Japanese and Chinese interests. While Japan wants a stable China, most Japanese leaders harbor a private concern that a militantly nationalist China may ultimately cast a longer shadow over Asia than is desirable. Chinese authorities also have their own apprehensions. The spector of a resurgent militarism that combines with Japan's economic prowess to project that nation swiftly onto the Asian stage in a manner reminiscent of old is not absent from the Chinese (and Southeast Asian) mind.

If Sino-Japanese relations have a political-strategic threshold beyond which they will not go, can the same be said of Sino-Soviet relations? When the alliance between the Soviet Union and China was consummated at the outset of China's Communist era, it was rightly signaled as one of the major events of the twentieth century. Yet after a decade, the two Communist giants split, and bitter public quarrels ensued. The process of Sino-Soviet normalization got under way, however, once the Chinese intitiated a shift during the 1980s toward nonalignment, hence distancing themselves from both of the superpowers.

Two concerns manifest themselves in the Soviet analysis of China and its future. One—shared by many other foreign observers—is whether or not political stability will be maintained in the post-Deng era, and precisely what political-economic course new leaders will take. Beyond this, however, many Soviets look to the longer-range future with a certain foreboding. There has long been an emotional fear of "the yellow peril" among the broad mass of Russian people. A reverse current of similar nature runs in China.

Two considerations are uppermost in the minds of Chinese policymakers today: development and security. The Soviet contribution to Chinese development, while not apt to be negligible, will fall well below that of Japan and the West unless conditions change radically. Current Chinese leaders look primarily to the latter sources for ideas, training, and advanced technology. There is little likelihood of a greatly reduced Soviet military presence in the near vicinity of China, and future Chinese leaders are as likely as those of the present to see this as either a constraint or a threat. In the light of these facts, it is improbable that a broad ideological and systemic similarity between these two states will be sufficient to knit them together politically.

What course are Sino-American political relations likely to take? The United States pursued a path of normalization with China in part because of the opportunity made available by the widening Sino-Soviet split of the late 1960s. With additional reasons in hand, rapprochement between the two countries proceeded steadily, although not without problems. The cultivation of strategic cooperation with China rapidly followed, and for a time, it was reciprocated. No less a person than Deng Xiaoping called for a global coalition to oppose Soviet hegemonism. Yet as the 1980s got under way, support for a strategic coalition was dropped, and the new theme was "nonalignment." China expects far more from the United States than from the Soviet Union in connection with its modernization drive. The fact that the United States poses no security threat to China is of at least equal importance and explains why Chinese leaders are still prepared to seek a low-level security relationship with Washington. Common interests—and mutual apprehensions of the USSR—override differences and sustain a relationship that is still expanding and that could have a decisive influence on the entire Pacific-Asian area.

It remains to examine the political relations between the United States and the Soviet Union as they pertain to Northeast Asia and then to explore the relative position of the two superpowers in their competition for influence within the region as a whole. The success of the current Soviet approach to Asia is likely to hinge on whether Moscow is prepared to make basic changes in political-strategic policies while at the same time expanding its economic relations on a substantial scale. As yet, there is little evidence to suggest that Soviet leaders are able to take such a course.

The political position of the Soviet Union in Northeast Asia remains weak despite the gains of the recent past. The USSR is less well situated politically than was the case thirty-five years ago when its alliance with China seemed firm, North Korea was a client state, and Japan scarcely counted. With few exceptions, its Asian neighbors have found the Soviet Union overbearing. Beyond this, neither the Soviet political structure nor its economic system serves as a model at this point in history.

What are the concrete implications of the fact that the Soviet Union comes to Asia today without its earlier political advantages? Socialist idealism has been replaced by the search for workable programs, and an international socialist community under Soviet guidance no longer attracts adherents. The Soviets must now make its way in Asia—and in the world at large—as another nation-state, militarily powerful but in most other respects belonging to the great body of "developing nations," hence forced to learn more than to teach.

The Soviets can scarcely be happy with their position in Japan. In general, Soviet status in Japan is abysmally low. This applies to the Soviet approaches being made to China and the ASEAN bloc as well as Japan.

Virtually no progress has been made on issues of political-strategic importance to Beijing. Yet, the Soviet leaders have some reason to be satisfied. They now have less reason to fear a Sino-American strategic alliance against them, and they can envisage the possibility that either developments internal to China or some issue such as Taiwan might upset the still fragile Sino-American relationship. Moscow has grown increasingly concerned about what it labels a strategic entente among the United States, Japan, and South Korea—a development regarded as a further projection of American power against the vulnerable Soviet Far East.

When one compares the political position of the United States and the Soviet Union in Northeast Asia, there can be no doubt of American primacy. The more serious problem lies in the fact that the Soviet Union has little to offer the states of Northeast Asia politically. The United States faces a different set of problems. Political ties with most of the governments of the region range from reasonably good to excellent with the exceptions of Mongolia and North Korea. And the image of the United States among the articulate citizenry of aligned states is as positive as that of any foreign society. However, the United States is held to standards that are incomparably higher than those applied to the USSR. It can be said that the United States reciprocates these sentiments by insisting on higher standards for the countries of Northeast Asia than do the Soviets. The human rights issue in U.S. foreign policy exemplifies this process.

The role of human rights in U.S. foreign policy, however, is destined never to be resolved in a manner that will satisfy all Americans—or those governments with which the United States is associated. Some forms of U.S. pressure can be effective with authoritarian allies. Governments dependent in some degree upon U.S. aid and protection must be caused to recognize that the American people and Congress will not easily countenance sacrifices for causes which they do not believe in or on behalf of leaders whose values and capacities they have grave doubts, unless the security of the United States itself is directly involved. The human rights issue, therefore, has long rendered U.S. political relations with countries like South Korea and Taiwan complex.

The Strategic Configuration Centering Upon Northeast Asia

It is now commonplace to assert that regional and global strategic issues are intertwined, but nowhere is this more evident than with respect to Northeast Asia.

The Soviet Union emerged from World War II badly battered. Yet in a few years, Moscow presided over a vast empire, controlling all of East Europe and portions of Asia larger in size than those held at the height of Czarist power. In addition, the Soviets had acquired a new ally of great importance, China. Today, between one-third and one-fourth of total Soviet military strength is positioned east of the Urals, representing a dramatic surge of Soviet power in this region since the early 1960s. This surge in military power in part reflects tensions with the Chinese as well as a growing concern over the increasing economic power of pro-Western states in Northeast Asia.

Meanwhile, the United States is forced to ponder its own strategic priorities and policies in a rapidly changing international environment. Shortly after the close of World War II, the United States established commitments that have remained intact for forty years. At an early point, it was realized that East Asia would play a steadily greater role in determining the global balance, economically and politically as well as militarily. While it was easy for American policy-makers to agree that the Pacific Asian theater was of vital consequence to American interests, it was far more difficult to reach a consensus upon the appropriate U.S. strategy for this region.

Recent American strategy in the Pacific Asian region has been an integral part of U.S. global strategy. The United States, however, cannot expect to match the Soviet military strength in East Asia quantitatively. Since U.S. strategy is centrally geared to its global power and specifically its nuclear capacity, it must depend much more heavily upon the conventional capacities of its allies than is required of the Soviets. Hence, the United States must be deeply concerned about the political and economic health of those states with which it is aligned. Instability within key Asian states may well constitute the gravest threat to security within the region.

Whatever the facts, it is a widespread assumption in Asia that the two superpowers have achieved a rough strategic equivalence both in the Pacific Asian region and globally. Hence, it is presumed that neither will take the risk of attacking the other and that sooner or later, a new strategic arms limitation agreement will be achieved. Meanwhile, virtually every Asian state is inclined to regard the Soviet Union as essentially an American problem.

What generalizations can be drawn from the strategic policies and relations of the major powers as they apply to Northeast Asia? First, despite some zones of tension, notably the divided states, East Asia is unlikely to be the seedbed of a global war, although this does not preclude its involvement in a conflict which is not promptly contained. Second, the simple balance of weaponry—conventional and nuclear—favors the USSR in the Northeast Asia theater, but when the full range of factors is taken into account, the Soviets have reason to be less than satisfied with their position. Strategically and politically, they stand virtually alone, whereas the United States has a network of meaningful ties with the most important Northeast Asian states. Third, while security ties of a regional nature have grown in Northeast Asia, a regional security structure along the lines of NATO or the Warsaw PACT countries is not remotely possible at this point or in the near future. Thus, the burdens upon the United States will be disproportionately heavy, and this may cause further strain. Fourth, despite the importance of a broad strategic equilibrium, security for most Northeast Asian states will be increasingly related to their internal economic and political health. In the future as in the past, domestic upheaval is the surest route to external intervention.

Reflections on U.S. Policy in Asia

Are there lessons for U.S. policy toward Asia in the foregoing analysis? First, the greatest obligation on the part of the United States is to put its own economic house in order. Second, we must make a sustained effort to reach an agreement with the Russians on strategic arms limitation that turns us away from further escalation of the arms race. Third, we have every right to expect the nations aligned with the United States to do more on behalf of themselves and on behalf of the region they inhabit, not merely with respect to security but also in economic and political terms. Fourth, in the coming age of alignments rather than alliances, the United States should foster a range of private instruments of discussion and consultation to augment the public bodies that exist. Fifth, East Asia is ready for a series of loose Pacific Asian forums, economic and social in nature. The basis for a tight, formal regional structure currently does not exist and is not likely to come into being soon.

One final comment seems in order. If the problems confronting East Asia and the major powers so intimately involved in the region seems formidable, the opportunities for pioneering ventures in economic, political and strategic cooperation are also extensive. The human and natural resources of the Pacific Asian area make it the logical pace-setter of the century ahead. And with its future, the future of the United States is inextricably connected. Our priorities and our policies must reflect that fact.

I. Introduction

The geopolitics of Northeast Asia has changed dramatically in modern times. In the not distant past, this was one of the more remote areas of the world. After experiences with the bearers of Christianity proved divisive, Japan's rulers pursued an exclusionist policy that kept all but a handful of foreigners away from that society's shores for more than two hundred years. Across the straits of Tsushima, the medieval kingdom of Korea enforced isolation with even greater rigor, earning the appellation, "Hermit Kingdom." To the north, Siberia remained a barren region inhabited largely by nomadic peoples—hunters, herders and fishermen. Interspersed were a small number of Russian forts, outposts in a vast, disputed wilderness. To the south lay China, the heartland of Confucian culture. But as the nineteenth century dawned, the Celestial Kingdom also sought to protect itself from the intrusions of the Western barbarians with policies stressing aloofness.

If the Westerner was unwelcome throughout the region, relations among the peoples within Northeast Asia were only slightly more congenial. Enmity was already a pronounced feature of Japanese-Korean relations, primarily as a result of Hideyoshi's abortive effort to conquer the Korean peninsula. And although China had had a great influence at earlier points throughout East Asia, its reach by the nineteenth century was largely restricted to Korea, and even there, contested as the century drew to a close. The Treaty of Nerchinsk, concluded in 1689, fixed one border between the Russian and Chinese empires, but nothing approaching cordiality or intimacy was to develop between the two peoples and governments.

Thus, less than two centuries ago, Northeast Asia was characterized by remoteness from the power centers of the early modern world and xenophobia. Advanced cultural zones and high levels of premodern agricultural productivity existed in the heartlands, but the challenges that provided the impetus for Western science and technology were absent. Geography, however, is unable to impose a fixed, timeless condition on a society or region. Today, Northeast Asia is at the very vortex of that vast area that we call Pacific Asia, a part of the globe destined to shape the twenty-first century economically, politically and strategically.

Economic relations within the region are intense and unbalanced—a volatile combination. Yet few doubt that Northeast Asia together with its major trading partners will set the economic pace for the rest

1

of the world and, in the process, determine the relative degree of competition versus cooperation, self-reliance versus interdependence with which we all shall live.

Politics, however, will remain an independent variable. The states of Northeast Asia may be defined to include both the United States and the Soviet Union, and in the northern Bering Sea these two nations are within walking distance of each other. Together with Japan and China, the United States and the USSR constitute the "big four" of the future, the nations most likely to determine global issues of war and peace and, apart from this, to affect the course of organizational efforts beyond the nation-state.

Progress in these directions is made more complex because these states and the broader region of Northeast Asia within which they interact represent the three types of political structure most typical of our age: the democratic, Leninist, and authoritarian-pluralist systems. Within each of these categories, differences of political style and operational mode abound. Thus, the two democratic nations, the United States and Japan, operate similar political institutions very differently, reflective of the unique cultural antecedents and historical evolution of the two societies.

Even more significant may be the political distinctions that appear to be developing between the two large nations flying Leninist banners, the Soviet Union and China. Once again, while ideology and political structure provide important elements of commonality, differences of culture, timing of emergence into the world stream and stage of economic development combine to produce significant differences of attitude and policy. Moreover, these differences seem to be growing rather than diminishing.

Categorization or prediction concerning the diverse authoritarian-pluralist systems is a hazardous task. Broadly speaking, these are societies where a restrictive, elitist political structure coexists with and holds power over a pluralist socioeconomic order. South Korea and Taiwan are current examples in Northeast Asia, representing a tiny sample of a system that in its many variations is dominant throughout the so-called Third World. At some point, tension tends to build between the relatively traditional polity and the dynamic socioeconomic order in such societies. Political instability grows, although unilinear projections portray too simple a picture; retreats from and advances toward elitist-proclaimed political goals are commonplace, with economic and social conditions critical variables. At times of serious instability, however, the society becomes a target of opportunity for external forces, acting either defensively or from a perceived chance to expand influence. Thus, in the trauma of development implicit in their internal contradictions, the authoritarian-pluralist states have come to play a central, albeit often indirect role in the international politics of our times.

In Northeast Asia, an additional political complexity presents itself. This area is host to two divided states: North-South Korea and China-Taiwan, a situation that affects both the political and strategic calculations of the big four. It is sobering to realize that none of the states divided as a result of World War II or its aftermath, with the exception of Austria, has been unified peacefully. Vietnam was unified by force and now seeks to unify Indochina in a similar manner. Germany remains divided by international agreement, with diverse effects upon the German people. Both Korea and China-Taiwan continue to be divided without international agreement and therefore remain recurrent sources of tension, international as well as domestic.

Beyond the problems of political uncertainty and divided states, Northeast Asia shares an important trait with Europe: it is an area where regional and global security issues are inextricably intertwined. Since both the United States and the Soviet Union, the world's two superpowers, consider Northeast Asia virtually as critical as Europe to their overall strategic position, military force dispositions have a dual purpose or, in some cases, separate purposes, depending upon the nature of the weaponry. Hence, every other state of the region is uncomfortably aware that its own security and that of the two superpowers cannot easily be separated. As in Europe, this creates domestic controversy, and it underlines the fact that the relative strength of a nation or a group of aligned states must be measured in economic and political as well as military terms.

II. Economic Aspects of Major Power Relations

It is logical to turn to the economic dimension of major power relations first, since the role of economics in international relations has reached new levels of importance and continues to rise. To appreciate economic relations among the principal states of Northeast Asia at present, one must be aware of the basic economic trends affecting the region as a whole. Four important developments can be observed. First, in recent years, Northeast Asia has exhibited an economic dynamism attracting global attention. While growth rates have generally slowed—China being a prominent exception—the prospects are that if world conditions do not seriously worsen, Northeast Asia will continue to be an economic pacesetter.

Second, the societies enjoying the most rapid economic growth have followed the model pioneered by Japan, albeit with suitable variations. Even those societies such as China and North Korea that initially adopted a different developmental strategy are now committed to substantial modifications in former policies as they seek to avoid stagnation and obsolescence.

Third, despite the importance of indigenous conditions and policies, the two economic superpowers, the United States and Japan, have been and will continue to be critical to the course of economic developments in the region. The good health of the American and Japanese economies will support the optimism that currently holds sway regarding Asia's future; conversely, a sharp, sustained downturn in these key economies would have seriously adverse repercussions here and elsewhere.

Finally, a spreading and deepening network of economic ties has been built within Northeast Asia, with Japan as the primary catalyst. This network, which transcends ideological-political lines, represents the single most significant development of the post-1945 decades, one likely to produce increasingly important byproducts with the passage of time. Let us turn to a further exploration of each of these trends, then examine the manner in which the major powers relate to them.

For the market economies of Northeast Asia, the two decades after 1960 were generally a period of extraordinary growth. Such societies as South Korea, Taiwan and Hong Kong enjoyed average annual gross domestic product (GDP) real increases of 8-10 percent throughout these years. Japan, already a rising industrial power, had growth rates equally impressive, in the 7-8 percent range on average. The two Leninist societies of the immediate region, China and North Korea, had a more uneven record. In the case of China, political instability com-

4

bined with inept economic policies to restrain growth and cause it to take a very uneven course. North Korea, in addition to suffering from the weaknesses of a rigidly autarkic policy, was expending large sums in these years to maintain its military establishment. Both societies had shown rapid growth at earlier points by pursuing the Stalinist "big push" strategy, a set of policies calculated to boost industrial production swiftly. By the 1970s, however, an economic malaise was in evidence, one that is characteristic of autarkic, collectivist systems and manifest also in the Soviet Union. Hence, both societies—and more particularly China—have embarked upon reform efforts, spearheaded by the commitment to participate in the broader technological revolution taking place around them.

In the early 1980s, the growth rates of the newly industrializing countries (NICs) of Asia, popularly known as the little tigers, slowed. Questions were raised as to whether the policies pursued up to this point—particularly the heavy dependence upon the American market—could be successfully continued. But as the 1980s reached the midpoint, the economies of South Korea, Taiwan and Hong Kong had at least temporarily met the challenges of the times. Aided by a resurgent American economy, continued Japanese strength, and lower energy costs, they were posting real GDP growth at 5-8 percent. Japan's growth fluctuated around the 2.5-3 percent mark, with that nation still leading the industrial states' growth on a sustained basis. The Chinese economy, liberated from some of the past restraints, had galloped ahead, and now it had to be reined in to prevent further overheating and serious inflation. Goals were set at 7.5 percent for the near term. Meanwhile, the United States and the Soviet Union both belatedly began to take seriously their internal economic problems, with results as yet impossible to predict. Their growth rates promise to be close to the 2.5-3.5 percent level, toward the upper level if things go well.

Why has a small group of Northeast Asian societies set the economic pace for the world? Due credit should be given to the cultural factor. Without exception, these are societies that share a Sinitic cultural tradition. That tradition rests centrally upon an intricately structured family system that encompasses discipline, hierarchy and a strong work ethic. Beyond the family and clan, these societies have had experience with complex organizations, political and economic. The techniques of governance and of commercialism are well advanced. Underwriting the political-economic order, moreover, is a respect for education, the means whereby skills at all levels can be nurtured and transmitted.

Yet culture alone is clearly an insufficient explanation. The Asian societies that have achieved the strongest economic record have pur-

5

sued a similar economic strategy in recent decades. That strategy, initiated in the post-1945 period by Japan, can be outlined in relatively simple terms: import the necessary energy and industrial materials, taking advantage of low prices; produce a manufactured product geared to the markets of more advanced societies, taking advantage of both the price differential between raw materials and finished products and the prosperity of the Western industrial nations; concentrate not upon research frontiers but upon transferring known technology into high-quality, marketable products with the utmost speed, studying consumer desires in key markets; focus on market share rather than immediate profits, accepting the most marginal returns initially, if necessary; and, while relying heavily upon the private sector, cultivate a symbiotic relation between government and industry, with the former serving as supporter, facilitator and persuader, assisting and on occasion deterring via credit policies, protection in various forms and a broad set of economic and political measures that generally create a climate favorable to the indigenous business community.

Via these policies, first Japan and then—with modifications—Taiwan, South Korea and Hong Kong have achieved their economic "miracle." Each state has had its significant policy variations, the product of differing internal circumstances. The Hong Kong government, for example, has pursued an essentially laissez-faire policy toward industry except for certain controls in connection with property. Taiwan, largely for political reasons, has pursued foreign investment more actively. South Korea, on the other hand, until recently favored foreign borrowing, thereby accruing a sizable foreign debt. Japan has benefited from an extraordinarily high savings rate among its people, the result of both culture and policy. Nevertheless, the broad strategy outlined above has been followed with great success by each of these societies.

As indicated, the effectiveness of these policies has been highly dependent upon the availability of foreign markets, and recent statistics indicate without question that the critical market has been the United States. In 1984, the United States took more than one-third of the total exports of Japan and South Korea, 45 percent of those of Hong Kong and 50 percent of Taiwan's. Its share of the China market was only about 10 percent. In comparison, Japan was a distant second as a market for the goods of neighboring societies, in 1983 taking 14 percent of Korean exports, 11 percent of Taiwan exports, 5 percent of Hong Kong exports, but 20 percent of China exports. When the import figures of the four countries are examined, however, the relative importance of the United States and Japan is reversed. In each of the Northeast Asian NICs as well as in China, Japan accounts for approximately one-fourth of all imports. Every one of these societies,

6

moreover, currently runs a trade deficit with Tokyo. The ratio of American imports to total imports varies, but in no case does it reach the level of Japan, and none of these societies runs a trade deficit with the United States. On the contrary, the cumulative current-account deficit of the United States in Northeast Asia constitutes approximately one-half its present $170 billion deficit. With Japan alone, the deficit is likely to exceed $60 billion in 1986, efforts to provide remedial measures notwithstanding. Due to these and parallel trends elsewhere, the United States has become a debtor nation, and conversely, Japan has become a major creditor nation.

Regionalism—The Current Thrust

While the implications and duration of this situation continue to be debated, two somewhat contradictory developments have unfolded. On the one hand, Japan has been sharply criticized by virtually every one of its trading partners, accused of a variety of shortcomings or misdeeds: perpetuating a largely closed market despite the removal of formal barriers; dumping its products to eliminate competitors; reluctance to transfer technology or invest in those areas most useful to host countries; and undue conservatism with respect to foreign assistance.

On the other hand, notwithstanding these criticisms, Japan is the principal party to the emergence of a *soft* regionalism in Northeast Asia, with its central element a growing network of economic ties among virtually all of the societies of the region. It is a soft regionalism because it lacks a formal structure, but that makes it no less important. Japan is the linchpin because despite criticisms of amounts, balance and conditions, through its trade, credit, investments and technology transfer, it has forged strong bonds not only with South Korea and Taiwan, but also with China. Moreover, the current outsiders want to be included in the new economic orbit. North Korea has repeatedly signaled its desire to expand its economic relations with Japan. Soviet emissaries place renewed emphasis upon the economic base that can underwrite a new era in Soviet-Japanese relations.

While Northeast Asian regionalism is most strongly manifest in the economic realm, it is not devoid of political and even strategic components. Japanese leaders have long been cognizant of the charge that their foreign policy is merely one of market acquisition, their behavior that of economic animals. Using the economic foundations now established, Japan has cautiously injected political notes into its relations with South Korea and China. With equal caution, it exchanges intelligence of strategic value with the ROK and the PRC through various channels. More importantly, it accepts the fact that it is required to

7

play a role in regional defense as an inextricable aspect of the defense of Japan itself. There will be more discussion concerning these matters at a later point.

In all of these respects, regionalism has emerged, albeit with the elements of tentativeness, diffusion and an absence of formal structure prominent in the scene. While Japan is the principal catalyst, moreover, the growth of Northeast Asian regionalism is to be seen in the development of informal ties between China and South Korea, and among China, Hong Kong and Taiwan, as well as in the long-standing formal relations between China and North Korea and the recent resurgence of Sino-Soviet relations. To these, one could add the sporadic dialogue between North and South Korea and the strengthening of Soviet-North Korean ties.

In sum, a rapid increase of relations between and among the states of this region is taking place, even where strong ideological and political barriers remain. This process may be defined as one of Asianization. It is a development that meets with stiff resistance and countercurrents. At this point, moreover, it is primarily a product of policy-making elites with uncertain citizen support. Yet it represents a difference not merely in degree but in kind from the conditions of earlier decades.

The Primacy of Japan's Ties with the United States

Notwithstanding its growing involvement in this new trend, Japan retains as its central international commitment the relationship with the United States, and in general, that is reciprocated. At first glance, the overall strength of the American-Japanese alliance and its perseverance amidst adversity seem surprising. Two nations more different in culture and geopolitical circumstances would be hard to find. Opposites, to be sure, sometimes attract each other in politics as in individual encounters. Yet neither Japan nor the United States has come easily to an enduring alliance with another country. Despite its advent as an international economic power, Japan remains in many respects a closed society, with separateness and aloofness pronounced characteristics. The privateness of the Japanese, as individuals and as a society, stands in marked contrast to the extroverted nature of Americans as a people. Nor need one rest with psychology. In determining its national interests, the United States has historically placed strong emphasis upon self-sufficiency and the priorities that should be accorded domestic issues. Thus, after forays into the world justified in the name of moral imperatives, retreats to home and hearth have frequently followed. Even today, despite radically altered global conditions, that instinct survives.

Beyond these general considerations, there are the specific issues, most of them economic in nature, that create the current American-Japanese tension. We are in a delicate period, and deeper crises cannot be ruled out. Charges and countercharges are being leveled, and in truth, the faults are not on one side alone. The principal complaints are set forth below, first as voiced by the American critics, using their language.

Despite repeated pledges and six "market-opening" packages, the Japanese domestic market remains very restricted to industrial products from the United States and all other foreign countries. When the terms are equal, American products can compete. For example, where fair competition exists, U.S. semiconductor industry products outsell those of Japan at a ratio of five to one in Europe, and two to one elsewhere. In Japan, such items have been frozen out by various means. In agriculture also, restrictions abound, including those on forestry products. The excuse that Japanese tariffs are lower than those of most other industrial societies is not acceptable, since tariffs are not the primary means of restricting imports. The assertion that the problem is a cultural one will also not suffice since culture is used to rationalize practices not acceptable if a reasonable trading system among nations is to prevail.

In addition, Japan, along with certain other countries, regularly engages in dumping, namely, selling products abroad below the cost of production, pursuing this tactic until it has garnered a major share of the market. And only when retaliatory measures are threatened does the Japanese government begrudgingly respond with pledges and remedial steps—steps that turn out to be palliatives rather than genuine reforms.

The Japanese criticisms are equally severe. Certain quarters in the United States, it is said, are using Japan as a scapegoat to conceal the mismanagement of the American economy and the decline of American competitiveness. Japan now has lower tariffs than Western Europe or the United States, but even if all remaining tariff restrictions were removed, it would affect the trade balance only marginally. A major share of the problem lies in the huge U.S. fiscal deficits, high interest rates and the overpriced American dollar that prevailed until recently. The American trade deficit has been not merely with Japan but with a wide range of countries. Under the circumstances, moreover, the infusion of Japanese and other foreign capital into the United States is essential to sustain the American economy; in effect, Japan is enabling Americans to live beyond their means.

Further, the United States partakes of the welfare-state malaise characterizing Western Europe. Labor productivity has lagged even as wages have shot up. American management is geared to quick profits

9

rather than market share—a strategic decision for which Japan cannot be blamed. And having been accustomed to a vast domestic market, American entrepreneurs have done little in foreign market research, rarely developing products attuned to overseas tastes and needs. Moreover, quality control -pioneered in the United States and borrowed by the Japanese -has slipped in the country of its origin, reducing American competitiveness still further.

Underlying these separate grievances and making remedial actions more difficult are deeply implanted attitudes or emotions on both sides, derivative from past and current sensitivities. It has been virtually impossible for the average Japanese or even for the elite to accept the fact that Japan is now a rich nation. The overwhelming majority of citizens think and act as if Japan were small, poor and vulnerable. Thus, the savings ratio remains extremely high, and the concept of sharing Japan's wealth with others is a difficult idea to accept. Hence, governmental efforts to expand the domestic market and to meet other criticisms of trading partners have been the products of external, not internal pressure. Such actions have been reactive and lacking in initiative. Consequently, they have had limited political advantages for Japan at the point they are begrudgingly made.

Yet at the same time, for a growing number of Japanese, pessimism and defensiveness have been modified by the pride taken in recent achievements and a rising annoyance at foreign criticism. A feeling of self-assurance that on occasion manifests itself in smugness, even arrogance, can be discerned.

On the other hand, the American mood has proceeded from a different base toward a different end. Accustomed in earlier times to being the sole preeminent power and able to provide for the international needy from the bountiful American largesse, the United States has suddenly found itself challenged militarily by the USSR and economically by Japan. Increasingly, moreover, Americans have felt the constraints of a complex global and domestic environment. From an American perspective, the world has become increasingly ungovernable, at precisely the time when American resources have become more restricted. And the needs at home have vastly increased. As a consequence, resentment against perceived unequal treatment and a demand for greater burden-sharing have grown apace. Two words graphically capture the recent American mood: fairness and reciprocity—an insistence that others not take advantage of the United States. Moreover, a rising American nationalism takes form in demands that more attention be paid to American problems, American needs and American rights.

Black clouds remain on the horizon. In the United States, protectionism in various forms continues to be hotly debated, and it may loom up as a key issue in coming elections. In Japan, stubborn political resistance makes the fulfillment of administrative pledges difficult. Despite the remedial measures that have now been taken on both sides, the situation may get worse before it improves. Yet in paying homage to these facts, one must not lose sight of one overarching trend. In spite of the conflicting moods and recurrent tensions, the United States and Japan are more closely interrelated today than at any time in history. Fierce competition, harsh repartee and repeated threats from Congress have not stifled a growing economic interdependence of profound significance for both societies. In 1986, two-way trade is likely to exceed $100 billion. A surge of Japanese investment is under way in such American industries as vehicles, electronics and steel. With more difficulty, American firms are now penetrating Japanese industries and financial institutions. Whatever its hazards—and they exist—this burgeoning interdependence is making old-fashioned protectionism obsolete. Protection for whom and against what?

Both nations moreover, with varying degrees of reluctance, are beginning to tackle the most pressing economic issues. Belatedly, the United States is seeking to reduce the annual budget deficits, even if an adequate solution to this problem has thus far proven elusive, with a continued resistance to increasing taxes or slashing defense expenditures. The overpriced dollar has been brought down significantly, although a far-reaching reform of the international monetary system is merely in the discussion stage, with no consensus in sight. The issue of competitiveness is also being given serious attention both in the private sector and in government. Meanwhile, an experiment with a new approach to trade grievances is under way, with market-oriented sector selective (MOSS) negotiations substituted for the old unfocused talks and penalties against specific trade violators in place of blanket protectionist legislation. These efforts are being aided by a strengthened American economy. The degree to which recent actions will alleviate the ongoing trade imbalance, however, remains in doubt. There are clearly no panaceas, and economists seem baffled by the recent behavior of the American economy.

If the critical need for the United States is to deflate its economy, that for Japan is to reflate, expanding its domestic market and, in the process, improving the quality of Japanese life. As American savings rates have been too low, those of Japan have been too high for the health of our mutual relations. Tentative steps in the direction of realigning the Japanese economy are being taken. Difficult U.S.-Japan negotiations have also produced certain modifications in testing and licensing procedures for American products, one of the many nontariff barriers to the Japanese market. Lying ahead is the vastly more difficult task of getting Japanese—citizens as well as entrepreneurs—to develop internationalist attitudes and policies, in the process modifying the highly restricted network within which the great bulk of Japanese domestic economic transactions take place. Some Japanese object, saying that this calls for cultural change, and so it does, but cultural change is in the nature of our times.

In broader terms, both Japan and the United States face the challenge of undertaking rapid, continuous structural changes in their economies that will enable them to keep pace with the global industrial revolution and the corresponding demands laid upon advanced industrial societies. It is now commonly recognized that we stand on the threshold of a new world, one in which the two economic giants must operate on the cutting edge of such fields as electronics, biotechnology, space and telecommunications. Ours is an age, moreover, when bilateral interaction must be accompanied by multilateral agreements both within and outside formal institutional arrangements. The economic regionalism so cautiously signaled at present in Northeast Asia and elsewhere in the Pacific-Asia area must be cultivated through diverse channels and in multiple ways. Globally, the General Agreement on Tariffs and Trade (GATT) negotiations have to be expanded, and efforts must continue to replace the defunct Bretton Woods agreement with a monetary policy that will provide greater stability, difficult though this will be.

In sum, Japan and the United States must both operate under one commandment: from strength flow the responsibilities for leadership in a world that cannot long tolerate economic anarchy. In our bilateral relations, meanwhile, we shall live with an ever-changing combination of competition and cooperation.

As has been indicated, however, the pivotal economic issues are not merely bilateral ones. Indeed, both Japan and the United States are at once the catalysts of and the threat to NIC development. Conversely, the latter societies in increasing measure present grave problems to both economic superpowers. From Taiwan, South Korea and Hong Kong comes a flood of goods onto the American market that has made deep inroads in competition with select American industries, thereby feeding protectionist sentiments. Many of the charges leveled against Japan, such as dumping, export subsidization and restricted domestic markets, are now directed against the NICs. Moreover, there is every reason to believe that the penetration of the American market by these countries and others moving into this category will rapidly increase, replacing Japanese as well as American products. Nor is the threat for Japan limited to the U.S. market. Such traditional Japanese industries as shipbuilding, steel and textiles now feel increasing pressure with respect to European and Third World markets from external producers with cheaper labor and equally modern technology.

At the same time, every Asian trading partner voices the same complaint against Japan as the United States—asserting that Japan's largely closed market contributes to their sizable trade deficits with that nation, creating an intolerable situation. Complaints do not stop with trade issues. Japanese entrepreneurs are described as ultracautious in technology transfer and unprepared to engage in investment in those fields most crucial to the balanced development of the interested country.

Japan's Economic Relations with China

It is precisely these criticisms that are voiced by officials of the People's Republic of China. On the one hand, as noted, Japan accounts for over one-fourth of China's foreign trade. In 1985, two-way Sino-Japanese trade reached $19 billion, although the trade figures for 1986 are uncertain due to China's foreign exchange restrictions. China's trade deficit with Japan in the first half of 1985 was a substantial $6 billion. Despite the fact that Japan will continue to be crucial to China's modernization drive, moreover, the Japanese private sector has shown a limited interest in transferring technology to China or in making investments in critical sectors of the Chinese economy in recent years. The concentration has been upon trade, and such high-pressure advertising techniques as billboards and television ads have been conducive to promoting a nationalist reaction. The recent student charges that "Japanese imperialism has reinvaded China" stemmed partly from such actions. The Chinese government does not share the students' call for a smaller Japanese presence, but faced with declining foreign exchange reserves, it has put pressure upon Japanese traders to accept "compensation trade"—namely, balanced trade through such practices as the purchase of products manufactured by plants exported to China by Japan.

Japan has had answers to the criticisms leveled against it from Beijing. The trade deficits of the recent past, Japanese spokesmen assert, have been in considerable measure the product of overzealous provincial authorities who were permitted to spend foreign exchange for consumer goods, in some cases reselling them at a handsome profit. The impetus thus came from within China, not primarily as a product of Japanese aggressiveness, and it has now been curbed by Beijing's fiat. Beyond this, China's import requirements are huge if its industrial revolution is to be speedily advanced, and Japan is the logical source for many of these needs. As for technology transfer, some Japanese do fear a boomerang effect whereby Chinese products, enhanced by modern technology and produced by cheap labor, will

13

challenge the Japanese in the regional and global marketplace. But the more substantial Japanese concern is that Chinese authorities find it difficult to accept the fact that technology is sold, not given away, and that for the most part it is the property of the private sector, with the necessity of striking a bargain that benefits both sides.

Investment in China has been approached cautiously, state Japanese entrepreneurs, because such crucial issues as profit repatriation and other safeguards or guarantees have not been resolved despite some progress in providing a legal framework for foreign investors. The vagaries of Chinese policies and the rapid, unforeseen changes that take place together with the multiple weaknesses of Chinese management and the labor force have plagued Japanese as well as other foreign entrepreneurs.

Despite the ongoing issues, however, Japan's economic relations with China are destined to grow. The Japanese commitment to the PRC is manifest in the investment being made in personnel training and information-gathering; in the concessional loans and other forms of Japanese governmental support; and in the willingness to make concessions others have not been prepared to make. For its part, moreover, China has been gradually moving to meet the primary complaints of foreign entrepreneurs and investors.

U.S.-PRC Economic Relations

American investors in China have had concerns similar to those of the Japanese without the same official support or private infrastructure. U.S. investment in the PRC to date has totaled only $700 million. Thus far, investment in China, for both Americans and Japanese, has been primarily a gamble on the future rather than a source of current profits. U.S.- China trade in 1985 came to approximately $8 billion, less than one-half that of Japan or of U.S.- Taiwan trade which reached $22.5 billion. PRC trade with both Japan and the United States has been hampered by the limited number of China's marketable products and the difficulties encountered by the key ones. The drop in oil prices has affected the value of Chinese exports to Japan, and the flood of foreign textiles into the American market place has prompted restrictions, limiting the rapid expansion of this trade. American exports to China have been largely concentrated in two areas: agricultural products and high-technology items, including those having actual or potential military applicability. Agricultural sales have been adversely affected, at least temporarily, by the increased Chinese production of food crops. Certain high-technology products confront COCOM regulations or raise concerns in U.S. domestic quarters, although some relaxation has recently taken place.

China's seventh Five-Year Plan for 1986-1990 paints official objectives in broad outline. Placing an emphasis upon manager initiatives and market forces, the government aims at an annual growth of 7.5 percent, with priority to be given to energy, transport and communications development. The intention is to curb excessive imports while increasing exports, insisting upon compensation trade in some form. It will still be necessary to increase foreign borrowing to reach the goals set. A drive is planned to train more technical school and university students so as to strengthen the weak managerial infrastructure.

The well-publicized goal of PRC leaders for the year 2000 has been to achieve a quadrupling of the 1980 gross output to $1 trillion and to raise national per capita income, which reached $450 in 1985, to $800. A recent World Bank report is cautiously optimistic but warns against efforts to push growth too fast, leaving the service sector underdeveloped. The report strongly supports greater reliance upon market forces, continued decentralization and the encouragement of foreign investment, thereby sanctioning the general direction signaled by the ongoing reforms.

The large questions pertaining to China's economic future are easy to pose but difficult to answer. Will political stability continue in the post-Deng era, and will a sufficient consensus supportive of the general economic course now being pursued be maintained to prevent abrupt changes? Or to put the latter portion of the question differently, will the policies now in effect and being projected into the future work sufficiently well to subdue critics and retain public support?

Answers to these questions vary, even within China. Ideological predilections, moreover, enter into the responses. Some Soviet observers, for instance, assert that the current Chinese experiments resemble the New Economic Policy inaugurated in the late Lenin era, albeit with the Chinese reforms going further and deeper. They insist that after a period of trial and error, Chinese economic policies will return essentially to the Soviet model, with the market strictly subordinate to a centralized, socialist structure. They add that this will enhance the opportunities for Sino-Soviet cooperation by providing a common ideological-systemic foundation.

Other observers, especially Americans, believe that despite problems, there will be no turning back. In its own unique manner, China will create a blend of planning and market-oriented enterprise which it will label "Chinese socialism." The needs of this hybrid economic system will cause the PRC to interact ever more closely in economic terms with Japan and the advanced West, although this will not preclude increased economic intercourse with the USSR.

Irrespective of China's future course, there can be broad agreement that the central issue is that of effectively integrating the three economies that currently coexist: the centralized, controlled economy; the decentralized, guided economy; and the market economy. In reality, Chinese progress and problems are less the result of detailed, careful planning than the product of general ideas initiated via campaigns that result in great bursts of energy and excesses that must subsequently be curbed. Thus, relaxation and tightening alternate in both economic and political realms, reminiscent of the contrasting yin-yang factors in traditional Chinese philosophy. Such a pattern seems destined to continue.

Under the best of conditions, moreover, Chinese modernization will be a protracted process, replete with an intricate mix of successes and failures. It will require sustained concentration, thus limiting China's foreign policy options. At the same time, a nation that will have a population of 1.2 billion people by the early twenty-first century will loom large within Asia in every respect. And despite all of the attendant problems, Japan, China and the United States will almost certainly be involved in an expanding, increasingly intricate economic relationship. China's spiraling economic needs and desires, moreover, have already engendered a growing economic relation with South Korea and Taiwan, albeit on an unofficial basis. That too will expand, although not necessarily without interruptions. While ideological and political boundaries will continue to restrain, they will not block the emergence of a new economic community.

Japan-USSR Economic Relations

Will the Soviet Union become a significant participant in the economic future of the Pacific-Asian region and, more especially, in Northeast Asia, or is it destined to be largely peripheral to coming developments, as has been the case in the recent past? It is common knowledge that the Soviet Far East contains large energy, mineral, and marine resources, and that the exploitation of these resources has long been on the Soviet agenda. Vast in area, thin in population and with a forbidding climate, Siberia has proven more difficult and costly to develop than was earlier contemplated. The opening of this region will require many decades and very substantial funds, in competition with the monies badly needed for the modernization of the USSR's industrial heartland. External assistance will be important, and already Japan has been willing to make modest investments.

Once again, economic logic would suggest that Japanese-Soviet economic cooperation could be beneficial to both parties, with Japan providing sophisticated high technology products and capital, receiving energy, mineral and forestry products in return. Gorbachev signaled this hope again in his well-publicized Vladivostok speech of July 28, 1986. Whatever the elemental logic in such an arrangement, however, serious obstacles exist at present. The political-strategic impediments are obvious. At a time when the Soviet Union has greatly increased its military installations and weaponry in Northeast Asia, assistance in the development of Soviet transport, communications, and an industrial infrastructure within the region not only would add to Japan's own security problems, but would arouse strong resentment in both China and the United States.

Economic considerations also provide limits. When Japan declined to assist in the development of the Tuymen petroleum fields in the 1970s, it was partly because the private sector did not find the Soviet proposal economically attractive, and that is not the only instance of this problem. Japanese involvement in Soviet Far East development has included port renovation, the timber industry, and the natural gas project in Sakhalin—a project that is likely to attract sustained Japanese interest. It should be noted, however, that in the past decade, through energy-raw material conservation measures and a movement to technology- and knowledge-intensive industries, Japan has lessened its need for some of the resources that the Soviet Far East has to offer. Fishery agreements represent a tie of significance, especially to Japan, a country now hard pressed to maintain its fishing industry in the light of mounting restrictions applied by diverse states. But the Soviets cannot be expected to be overly generous in such arrangements. As in the case of China, the central problem for the USSR is that of generating foreign exchange, finding products that Japan will buy in exchange for its industrial commodities. This problem is made more complex because of the Soviet necessity of satisfying its European trading partners. If, as seems likely, strong pressure for compensatory trade is applied similar to the Chinese position, the Japanese capacity to respond favorably will be limited.

To the extent that the Gorbachev era witnesses a general economic revitalization of the Soviet Union, however, including the acquisition of an assorted range of high technology, Japan will strive to participate. Already, numerous Japanese firms are represented in Moscow, and bidding on various projects is active. Since the Japanese embargo imposed after the Soviet invasion of Afghanistan in 1979 was lifted, moreover, sales of products like computers have taken place. While the prospects for intensive Japanese-Soviet economic interaction are clearly limited in the short term, longer-range possibilities should not be discounted. The variables that will determine this are both political-strategic and economic. It would not be surprising, however, if at some point in the early twenty-first century, developments in the two countries reach a stage promoting an expanding economic interaction.

Sino-Soviet Economic Relations

If Japan offers the Soviet Union long-term possibilities with respect to both Siberia and the more general modernization of the Soviet economy, economic relations with China provide the Soviets with the chance for immediate gains, political as well as economic. From a very low level, Sino-Soviet trade is now growing rapidly. It still represents a negligible quotient of the total trade of both countries, having reached only about $2 billion. Nevertheless, the reestablishment of a vigorous border trade, the Soviet commitment to modernize certain Chinese plants built by them in the 1950s, and the renewed training of Chinese technicians in the USSR all point to gradual normalization of Sino-Soviet economic relations despite Beijing's denial that true normalization can take place until the three obstacles relating to Vietnam, Afghanistan and Soviet border troops are removed. Among the most interesting proposals advanced by Gorbachev at Vladivostok were those of resolving the Amur river boundary between the USSR and the PRC on the basis of the main shipping channel, thereby basically acceding to the Chinese position, supporting joint water management projects, and assisting in building a railroad to connect Kazakhstan and Xinjiang—steps that would facilitate trade in addition to reducing tension.

It remains to be seen how extensive Sino-Soviet economic relations will become. The Russian argument is that given the Chinese system, now and in the future, managers and technicians trained in the USSR can be integrated at home with far less disruption than those trained in Japan or the United States. Current Chinese leaders, however, in addition to remembering the 1950s with decidedly mixed emotions, show a pronounced preference for the technology of Japan and the West. In general terms, the latter countries are seen as more modern than the Soviet Union. Rightly or wrongly, the Chinese want to emulate the vanguard, as has been the case since this proud people were first forced to deal with the external world. If Sino-Soviet trade is carried out on a barter basis, moreover, natural limitations will continue to make themselves felt. Thus, barring political developments in China highly favorable to the USSR, Sino-Soviet economic intercourse, while continuing to increase, will not keep pace with Beijing's interaction with the advanced market economies.

The Economic Component in U.S.-USSR Relations

Finally, there is little likelihood that Soviet-American economic relations will greatly expand in the foreseeable future. Once again, if sheer economic logic were to apply, with certain modifications one might foresee the possibilities suggested with respect to longer-term Soviet-Japanese economic relations. Trade expansion, especially between Siberia and the west coast of the United States, has long been contemplated. Yet in addition to the current political-strategic barriers, economic complications present themselves, at least in the short run. American grain sales, one of the principal U.S. exports to the USSR, are now troubled by declining world prices. High-technology sales are restricted for strategic reasons. And there remains the question of what the Soviets can sell to the United States assuming that they are unwilling to accept an unbalanced trade financed by loans or other means. Should U.S.- USSR confrontation be progressively moderated and a series of agreements on the strategic and political fronts be realized, economic intercourse between the two military superpowers might improve, both directly and through third parties. But this is not in the immediate offing.

Soviet Options

The Soviet government has good reason to seek new policies in East Asia, policies that will supplement military power with more dynamic economic and political programs designed to induce Asian cooperation. Thus, the recent overtures for expanded trade and other forms of economic interaction proffered by Soviet representatives traveling in Asia have political value for Moscow in addition to whatever economic merit they may contain. Together with the plans to invite a larger number of Asians to study in the USSR and an expansion of other cultural exchanges, they represent an acknowledgment that the USSR has long needed a more sophisticated Asian policy. Even modest economic gains will be useful in promoting a new atmosphere for the Soviet Union. The Soviet request to participate in GATT is another sign of the desire to take part in greater degree in the international economy. But the results are not likely to be dramatic, and in the middle to long term, the Soviet capacity to interact in meaningful economic terms with the Pacific-Asian region will hinge upon the scope and depth of economic reforms within the Soviet Union itself.

Is it possible that the Soviet leaders will take a leaf out of the Chinese book, disclaimers to the contrary? Can one envisage the possibility that if efforts to make the system work better fail, Gorbachev and his new team will change the system itself? Will they dare to place a greater emphasis on the market and alter the autarkic elements in the economy significantly, thereby making possible a much more extensive interaction with the market economies of the world? The evidence to date is too scanty to permit any solidly based prediction. Skeptics abound and they may be correct, but the Soviet leaders' consciousness of problems has never been greater nor more openly expressed. If realism is followed by pragmatism, systemic changes of significance cannot be ruled out.

Conclusions

The survey of economic relations among the major powers in Northeast Asia lends itself to the following conclusions:

First, economic developments in this region seem likely to continue to be among the most dynamic in the world, granting that the course of the American and Japanese economies is a critical variable here as elsewhere. A broader caveat is also in order. The extraordinary fluidity marking economic conditions globally and regionally at this time, and the rapid shifts in national policies taking place or being contemplated, render even short-term predictions more hazardous than usual.

Second, economic growth in Northeast Asia is generally conducive to interdependence among the states of the region, underwriting a soft regionalism. The economic heartland consists of Japan, the United States, South Korea, Taiwan and Hong Kong, but China is being drawn progressively into this economic orbit as it reorients its system and redefines its goals. It will be increasingly more difficult for North Korea to maintain an autarkic system that is showing signs of obsolescence; for Pyongyang, moreover, increased economic contact with East Europe and the USSR may not suffice.

Third, the growing intensification of economic relations within the region and among the major states will exacerbate certain problems, posing major challenges as well as opportunities. These problems, moreover, will be progressively less susceptible to unilateral or bilateral resolution. Bilateralism will still have a prominent role to play, but the need for multilateral approaches will steadily grow. In addition to GATT and such agencies as the World Bank, the Asian Development Bank, and the International Monetary Fund, other cooperative efforts will be required, whether or not encased in a formal institutional structure.

Fourth, the most important bilateral relationship will continue to be that between the United States and Japan. The essence of that relation will be a dynamic mix of competition and cooperation operating under conditions of rapidly increasing interdependence. The premium will be upon both states being able to attune their domestic and international economic policies to the changing global environment. Their mutual responsibility for a workable economic order cannot be abdicated, although both states have every right to demand that others share that responsibility.

Fifth, China will be progressively interrelated with the market economies of this region, not only Japan and the United States but also the NICs. This will raise questions within China of a political and ideological nature, questions not likely to be resolved in the near term. But "Chinese socialism" will have unique characteristics, thereby supporting the staunch nationalism that is the foremost expression of late-twentieth century China. Meanwhile, of China's bilateral economic relations, that with Japan will be the most meaningful, but Chinese leaders, cognizant of past lessons, are not likely to accept too high a dependency on a single source.

Sixth, despite many barriers, the Soviet Union, and more particularly its vast Far East, will gradually be drawn into the Northeast Asian economic orbit. Like the western part of the United States, Siberia and the adjoining Soviet territories will develop an economic life partly distinctive to that region and, in the course of the twenty-first century, will find ways to participate more fully in the economic environment that surrounds them.

III. Politics and the Major Powers

The political dimensions of major power relations rival those in the economic realm in importance and complexity. The foremost task is to resolve or contain conflicts in perceived national interests and to adjust to major ideological-systemic differences. As noted, Northeast Asia contains three distinctive types of political systems: the democratic polity, the Leninist version of socialism, and the authoritarian-pluralist state. The effect that political variation can have upon intra-state relations should not be minimized. The structure of the state and the values attached to it influence the process by which decisions are reached as well as the content of those decisions.

One major trend of recent decades, however, has been the decline of ideology in virtually all of the major Pacific-Asian nations, as leaders grapple with problems on a pragmatic, experimental basis. For Japan, the zenith of the ideological era was reached in the 1930s when a mythological past was built into a rationale for a corporate state and regional dominance. Defeat in war ended old dreams. The Soviet Union was created by individuals in whose minds the vision of a unified socialist world burned brightly, but that vision had dimmed well before bureaucratic administrators like Khrushchev and Brezhnev came to power. For the first-generation Chinese Marxist revolutionaries, the goal was the liberation of both a people and a nation, but within the framework of the international socialist movement. Now, Maoism is in decline and Deng Xiaoping's query "Will it work?" dominates the scene. From its beginnings, the United States was suspicious of cosmic theories and prone to pragmatic approaches, albeit with an insistence that pragmatism rest on moral foundations.

In certain parts of the world, the decline of secular ideology has resulted in the reemergence of religion as a powerful political force. Fundamentalist Islam, Christianity, and Judaism have moved forward to answer the need for a set of values—a faith—that can sustain individuals in a time when old moorings are being swept away. For societies like China and Japan, however, with their Confucian background, religion has always played a lesser political role, although the Nichiren sect of Buddhism finds expression in the Kōmeitō, one of Japan's political parties. In Russia, some observers see a trend toward religious revival, but its extent is in debate. No one can doubt that in the United States, religious groups of various denominations have entered the political arena with growing impact. Yet the common denominator that can be most clearly identified in the four major Pacific-Asian states and that shows evidence of being on the ascendency is not politicized religion but nationalism.

Upon reflection, it is not surprising that nationalism continues to be the single most powerful political force in today's world, notwithstanding the growing interdependence among nations. In fact, nationalism is strengthened by the frustrations of interdependence. To be sure, one should not ignore the continuing vitality of localist or regional commitments. In few parts of the world has the nation-state become so dominant in the hierarchy of allegiance that adherence to all other levels of association has been obliterated. It can even be argued that in the United States under the Reagan administration, there has been a conscious effort to strengthen local and state institutions. In China also, attempts at decentralization proceed under very different conditions.

Nonetheless, the nationalist tides in both of these societies are running swiftly. In China in particular, Marxism-Leninism is being overwhelmed as its essential foreignness to Chinese culture is revealed, and both the government and the Communist Party are forced to rely ever more heavily upon nationalism. That has long been true in the Soviet Union, despite official paeans to Marxism. Even in Japan, where low-posture politics have been in vogue, a revitalized nationalism can be discerned. Here, as in South Korea, newer generations are imbued with the "can do" spirit, and their essential optimism about the future manifests itself in a variety of ways, including the type of self-confidence that brooks no individual or national slights. American nationalism, as noted, takes form in the determination to defend perceived U.S. interests and in a rekindled patriotism that runs deeply within the society. Thus, in exploring the political relations between and among the major states of Northeast Asia, one must take into consideration systemic differences and the common force of nationalism that characterize the scene.

This combination is conducive to a general trend of profound significance taking place in international relations, namely, the movement from alliance to alignment. At the end of World War II, both the United States and the Soviet Union created alliances that were tightly constructed, with the major power guaranteeing extensive military and economic support and receiving in return pledges of faithful allegiance. These alliances were highly exclusive, leading to the coinage of such terms as "camps." Outside of the alliance structure, a number of newly emerged states adopted a stance initially defined as "neutralist." Increasingly, in recent decades, relations between major powers and the states affiliated with them have been marked by a growing measure of fluidity. The guarantees of military and economic support by the major party, even where required, are less absolute, being generally couched in conditions and limited in nature, reflective of our nuclear age. On the other side, obedience or allegiance to the "bene-factor" has also become more conditional, with the quotient of inde-pendent action or separate, even conflicting positions rising.

It is thus increasingly appropriate to speak of alignments rather than alliances. As both the United States and the USSR have discov-ered, moreover, the successful management of alignments is vastly more complex than that of the earlier alliances. It requires a capacity for compromise, an acceptance of difference, and, above all, a willing-ness to consult and to develop genuinely collective policies. This is in strident contrast to the unilateral, often preemptive decision-making that superpowers have been prone to adopt, justified because of the degree of responsibility, including risks and costs, that they must accept in pursuing any given course of action.

No development is of greater importance to an understanding of international relations at the close of the twentieth century than the trend toward alignments, with all of the fluidity, complexity, and uncertainty that accompanies it. The term "multipolarity" has been used to describe our era, but while that concept has considerable validity, it is not wholly satisfactory either as a symbol or as a state-ment of fact. In sheer military terms, the world is more nearly bipolar than at any time in history. If both the United States and the USSR are frustrated in utilizing military power effectively, it is not because of new, challenging centers of military power, but because of both the expansion in the continuum of effective methods of applying violence to politics in our era and the changing nature of international relations at a time when the dependence-independence-interdependence mix in interstate relations is undergoing rapid, radical alterations.

The Political Foundations of the U.S.-Japan Relationship

In this context, the U.S.-Japan relationship has witnessed much less upheaval in political-strategic terms than most major power relations. Of all major American allies, Japan and Great Britain have been the most steadfast, being supportive of American positions in the great majority of instances and cautious in voicing differences when they existed. There are issues upon which the Japanese government holds views at variance with U.S. policy, such as the Middle East, but these differences have never been allowed to reach a point of public debate.

Why? The central reason is that the element of economic interde-pendence has dramatically increased while that of strategic depen-dency has remained high. Japan's dependence upon the United States for its security is a product of the 1947 constitution, which strictly lim-its the capacity of that nation to develop or use military forces except in cases that can be defined as self-defence in a strict sense. Japan

24

lacks a status granted to all sovereign nations, including the other powers defeated in World War II. It has thus remained dependent upon the United States to provide a nuclear umbrella and the other defense essentials. At the same time, economic trends in both nations have been conducive to a degree of interdependence in this sphere unprecedented among major nations with the possible exception of the European Economic Community.

Given this combination of strategic dependence and economic interdependence, the American-Japanese relation today is unique. As noted, this does not make it a wholly compatible relation. An additional factor fortifying the relation, however, is the broad measure of political agreement. This relates not merely to the fact that Japan and the United States hold common views on most political issues, especially those pertaining to Asia. It is also important that both societies share political values and institutions. In general terms, these two societies speak a common political language, although it would be a mistake to ignore certain significant differences. For example, the Japanese government, like most governments elsewhere in Asia and in Europe, does not agonize over the human rights issue to the same extent as the United States. While not devoid of compassion, Japanese officials formulate policies primarily on the basis of economic and strategic considerations. They do not expect the majority of societies with which they deal to exemplify liberal ideals, nor do they demand it. They eschew the role of serving as social engineers for others. Segments of the Japanese press and the opposition parties raise human rights issues selectively, but the government is invariably cautious except under egregious provocation such as the kidnapping of Kim Dae Jung, the South Korean oppositionist, on Japanese soil.

It would be foolish to assume that the present relation with the United States is fixed in perpetuity or that Japanese foreign policy will remain wholly unchanged. The debate over Japan's appropriate role in the world is certain to intensify. For some time, there have been three broad visions of a Japanese future, visions harbored by different elements within that society. The concept of a pacifist Japan was initially fostered by the American Occupation. In modified form, it has been carried forward by the Japan Socialist Party and sundry other idealists. Today, it is the vision of a Japan nonaligned and with minimal defense forces, prepared to interact equally with all nations in economic and cultural terms. Military ties would be avoided, with Japan's security resting upon international agreements together with the fact that Japan could threaten no one. Although this vision in its pure form has lost much of its lustre, even to the Socialists, in more diluted form it has a continuing appeal. Many Japanese are content with a low-posture foreign policy and see no need for an expanded Japanese role or binding ties to the United States.

A second vision at the opposite end of the spectrum is encapsulated in the concept of a Gaullist Japan, a nation emerging as a major power not merely in economic but also in political-military terms. Only under those conditions, it is argued, will Japan acquire the respect due it and, more importantly, a voice in the critical decisions that will affect its future along with that of other nations. Why should Japan be virtually ignored in all but economic matters, while much weaker nations like China are accorded global prestige? Gaullism in various forms has been growing, yet up to the present, a majority of Japanese are not willing to pay the costs and take the risks of such a policy. Critics, moreover, query whether Gaullism has been successful in terms of its original objectives in France, the country of its origin.

A third vision is less dramatic. It envisages a Japan remaining a part of the coalition led by the United States, with a greater measure of political consultation and joint security programs combining with heightened economic interdependence to provide Japan with a progressively larger measure of equality in the overall relationship. In exchange, Japan would accept expanded security responsibilities of a regional nature and the type of economic reforms conducive to lessened friction on this front, along with in-depth official and private exchanges designed to foreward agreement on key political issues. With occasional doubts and certain caveats, a majority of the Japanese electorate as well as most leaders support this vision. But the commitment is not so firm as to be unshakable if external conditions, including the policies of the United States, were to be radically altered.

In reality, there are portions of both the first and second visions in the changing mosaic that constitutes Japanese foreign policy, with the third vision dominant. Japan has moved cautiously to advance its political role by conducting in-depth discussions with Asian neighbors on those issues most vital to the region such as developments on the Korean peninsula. Such talks have been held with Chinese and American leaders as well as with the South Koreans, with messages derived from the conversations being communicated to other parties by Japanese sources. Facilitating this development have been the high-level visits, with Nakasone making trips to South Korea and China as well as frequent visits to the United States. Even a trip to the Soviet Union has been advanced as a possibility. In return, key leaders such as Reagan, Chun Doo Hwan, Hu Yaobang and Shevardnadze have made the trip to Tokyo, signaling the growing importance of Japan on the international stage.

Japanese political contacts have not been limited to these activities. Taking a leaf from the Communist book, the Japanese have created special organizations or used individuals to maintain discreet contacts with both North Korea and Taiwan. Liaison is not left to the opposition parties, although the Japan Socialist Party has ardently cultivated North Korea. The Liberal Democratic Party in effect has designated an individual within the party to be its link with Pyongyang and constantly tests the limits of Seoul's tolerance by permitting North Korean officials to visit Japan. The ties with Taiwan are much more extensive, with a sizable number of LDP figures keeping in touch with Kuomintang leaders despite Beijing's unhappiness with this dalliance. In the totality of these relations—official, semi-official, and unofficial—one can discern the expanding political reach of Japan, especially in Northeast Asia—another aspect of soft regionalism.

The Politics of the Japan-USSR Relationship

If Japan-U.S. political relations are strong at present, Japanese political relations with the USSR are at a low ebb. The principal obstacle on the Japanese side is the issue of the four northern islands. On this matter nationalist sentiments are clearly revealed, with unity among all Japanese political factions, from the most conservative factions within the LDP to the Japan Communist Party. Japan insists that these islands are an integral part of Japan, not an extension of the Kuriles, and are illegally occupied by the Soviet Union. With the passage of time and events these islands have come to assume a strategic as well as political significance. Viewing the basic U.S.-Japan objective as that of bottling the Soviet fleet inside the Sea of Okhotsk, Soviet officials want the maximum control of the off-shore islands, with a capacity to attack Japan from a close-in position and, if necessary, to occupy Hokkaido. Thus, Khrushchev at one point indicated that the USSR was prepared to return two of the islands to Japan in exchange for a peace treaty, but later, Soviet officials proclaimed that "the bus has left the station," thereby signaling that the proposal was no longer on the table. Indeed, in recent years, the Soviet position has been that no territorial issue between the USSR and Japan exists since the question of the islands has been conclusively settled. With equal insistence, Japanese spokesmen have asserted that until this issue is fairly resolved, there can be no peace treaty formally putting an end to the hostility between the two countries initiated by Moscow in the closing days of World War II.

One example of the Soviet effort to move toward a more flexible Asian policy has been the modest revision of its earlier position on the island issue. In the course of his January 1986 visit to Tokyo, Foreign Minister Eduard Shevardnadze accepted a formula whereby the Soviets acknowledge that the Japanese believe that the issue exists whereas the USSR asserts that the issue has been settled. Whether this slight concession augurs a gradual thaw in Japanese-Soviet relations is uncertain.

Were the Soviets to undertake a major policy shift by offering to return at least two of the four islands to Japan in exchange for modest Japanese concessions, it would undoubtedly cause divisions in Japan. While such a move would seem unlikely unless a very substantial quid pro quo were exacted, both Gorbachev and Nakasone have cogent reasons for wanting improvements in Japanese-Soviet relations. Soviet leaders would like to weaken U.S.-Japan ties; Nakasone and his colleagues do not want Japan to fall behind developments in Sino-Soviet and U.S.-USSR relations. Yet the depth of suspicion on both sides is profound and goes beyond officialdom. For nearly a century, Japan and Russia have been rivals in Northeast Asia, playing what at times was a zero-sum game. They have fought two declared wars and various other skirmishes, the most serious of which was the large-scale conflict on the Mongolian border in the late 1930s which resulted in thousands of casualties.

Polls reveal that the Japanese public has consistently regarded the USSR with the least favor of all foreign nations in recent decades, and more impressionistic evidence indicates that this attitude is reciprocated by Soviet citizens. Recent events in general fortify these sentiments. On a wide range of political-strategic issues from the Soviet invasion of Afghanistan and the downing of the South Korean civil airliner to the Soviet role in Indochina and the expansion of its military facilities both there and in Northeast Asia, Japan has viewed Soviet policies with apprehension and hostility. On the Soviet side, Japan is regarded as an appendage of American policy and power. Until recently, Moscow showed scant concern over Japanese feelings.

The Political Element in Japan-PRC Ties

At most, therefore, the improvement of Soviet-Japanese political relations is likely to be a slow, tortuous process, dependent in considerable measure upon trends in U.S.-USSR relations. Meanwhile, Japanese political relations with China have reached a stage that leaders on both sides characterize as "the best in this century." Here, the range of common interests has generally expanded. Japan's desire, like that of the United States, is for a politically stable, economically developing China. Both countries want to avoid another conflict on the Korean peninsula. Both have an interest in supporting ASEAN and opposing Vietnamese as well as Soviet expansion in Southeast Asia, although China has a greater intensity of feeling on the Vietnam issue than Japan. The two states hold similar positions on Afghanistan.

28

Yet one should not exaggerate the identity of Japanese and Chinese interests. While Japan wants a stable China, most Japanese leaders harbor a private concern that a militantly nationalist China may ultimately cast a longer shadow over Asia than is desirable. Hence, they hope that the developmental process in the PRC will be stretched out over a protracted period, with Beijing authorities preoccupied with the task of internal development for the foreseeable future.

Chinese authorities have their own apprehensions. The spector of a resurgent militarism that combines with Japan's economic prowess to project that nation swiftly onto the Asian stage in a manner reminiscent of old is not absent from the Chinese (and Southeast Asian) mind. Hence, efforts at textbook revision to alter the depiction of Japan's policies in the 1930s or Nakasone's visit to Yasukuni Shrine evoke strong protests. Although Beijing has endorsed Japan's efforts to develop an adequate self-defense, expecting its military forces to be pointed northward, there is no desire to see Japan take on broad military responsibilities in Asia.

Thus, the prospects for Pan-Asianism centering upon a Sino-Japanese alliance—long the dream of some and the fear of others—is a remote possibility. As indicated, Asianization, the intensification of a network of ties among the Asian states, will continue, and expanding Sino-Japanese bonds will be a part of that process. Yet Asian self-reliance is increasingly less feasible; the type of exclusiveness implicit in Pan-Asianism belongs to an earlier age, and even in that era it could never be realized, partly because the cultural as well as the political and economic differences between these two great Asian societies were always profound.

The Evolution of Sino-Soviet Relations

If Sino-Japanese relations, while destined to be of vital importance to both societies, have a political-strategic threshold beyond which they will not go, can the same be said of Sino-Soviet relations? When the alliance between the USSR and the PRC was consummated at the outset of China's Communist era, it was rightly signaled as one of the major events of the twentieth century. The fortunes of nearly one billion people had been politically linked, and if the alliance survived over time, the prospects for a Sino-Soviet condominium over the Eurasian continent seemed promising. Yet after a decade, the two Communist giants split, with bitter public quarrels ensuing. By the end of the 1960s, the cleavage had led not merely to ideological disputation and a severance of normal economic and political relations but to territorial issues that made large-scale conflict a distinct possibility.

What had produced this turn of events? Many specific causes can be cited: rivalry for authority in the post-Stalin era, and Chinese resentment at Soviet efforts to direct the policies of other socialist states; the Chinese turn away from the Soviet economic model; the unwillingness of Khrushchev to take risks of confrontation with the United States on behalf of Mao's campaign to seize the Nationalist-held offshore islands; and as a culminating, highly significant event, the Soviet retreat from the agreement to furnish China with nuclear technology. At root, the cleavage was a product of the fact that while these two states shared a common ideology and similar political institutions, they had profound differences of culture, stage of development, and degree of power. These differences translated into different perceptions of national interest. The consequent divergences of policies were given added impetus by the strong nationalist currents running in both societies and by the unique personalities of Nikita Khrushchev and Mao Zedong.

When Sino-Soviet relations reached their nadir with the 1969 conflict on the Ussuri River and the massive Soviet military buildup on China's borders, it was natural that Chinese leaders would seek drastic foreign policy revisions. Profoundly weak internally as a result of the inanities of the Cultural Revolution and isolated from the world, the PRC could neither negotiate nor fight with the USSR from strength. At this point, moreover, it was easy to realize that the United States held the key to China's reentry into the world. The suspension of a U.S. veto could permit PRC entrance into the United Nations. More importantly, a relaxation of U.S. strictures would allow rapid normalization of relations with Japan and various nations of West Europe, with both economic and political-strategic benefits.

Since the United States had its own reasons for pursuing the path of normalization, rapprochement between it and the PRC proceeded steadily, albeit not without certain problems. By the mid-1970s, the United States had achieved an enviable position, being able to interact effectively with both the USSR and the PRC at a time when Sino-Soviet relations remained frozen in hostility. Taiwan continued to be a persistent issue, but in the end it was finessed, despite the Beijing leaders' unhappiness when the Taiwan Relations Act was made a part of the normalization process. The broader strategic issue that divided the Carter administration related to the connection of China policy with American-Soviet relation. One view held that the United States should strive for a balanced relation with the USSR and the PRC, maintaining an equilibrium by advancing on both fronts in tandem. Thus, the ratification of SALT II and normalization of diplomatic relations with the PRC should go together, with both Communist nations subsequently being granted most favored nation status for purposes of trade. A contrary view held that a strategic relation with the PRC should be cultivated against the Soviet threat, thereby accepting—indeed welcoming—an unbalanced U.S. relation with the two major Communist states.

President Carter supported the first alternative until the Soviet invasion of Afghanistan, an event which placed the administration on the defensive against charges that both its security and diplomatic policies had been marked by naivete and softness. The cultivation of PRC strategic cooperation rapidly followed, and for a time it was reciprocated. No less a person than Deng Xiaoping called for a global coalition to oppose Soviet hegemonism.

Yet as the 1980s got under way, Chinese leaders undertook an abrupt and major change in PRC foreign policy. Support for a strategic coalition was dropped, and the new theme was "nonalignment," with spokesmen asserting that China would never participate in any military bloc. Rather, it would maintain its independence, identify itself politically with the Third World, and utilize its independent stance to criticize both of the superpowers when their policies "threatened peace, or were in violation of the rights of others." China itself would never act as a superpower, it was asserted, a pledge that Vietnam and certain other Asian states found difficult to accept.

It was in this context that the process of Sino-Soviet normalization began. Some observers have maintained that it was initiated at a time when grievances against the Reagan administration had accumulated and the prospects for further advances of U.S. ties seemed bleak. It is true that issues like Taiwan, trade, and technology transfer troubled U.S. relations with the PRC in the early Reagan years, but the more fundamental reasons for China's new foreign policy lay elsewhere, grounded in PRC domestic considerations. If the ambitious program of economic modernization were to be successful, it would require the greatest possible concentration of China's energy and resources. The government could not afford to spend vast amounts in maintaining and rapidly upgrading its military establishment. An alliance with the United States against the Soviet Union (or vice versa) would constitute a high-cost policy. Moreover, there were obvious advantages in occupying a position between the two superpowers, obtaining thereby a higher degree of flexibility and a certain capacity to play one off against the other.

In coming to these views, Chinese leaders could have been influenced by the diverse experiences of North Korea and Japan. Pyongyang had gained from its independent position—a position enabling it to play off the USSR and PRC, garnering assistance from both. Japan had been able to establish and maintain a low-cost, low-risk foreign policy, albeit by reliance upon the American defense commitment. It could be argued, of course, that the risk to Japan was rising, with the

Soviets mounting close-in military power. But for many decades, Japan had focused its resources overwhelmingly upon economic development, with spectacular results. Even without these examples, however, elemental logic could have led Chinese leaders to their new foreign policy.

Yet it should be noted that China's "nonalignment" rests heavily upon the maintenance of a basic strategic equilibrium both globally and in the Pacific-Asian region. In the 1970s, when that equilibrium was threatened by a relative decline in American power vis-á-vis that of the Soviet Union, the Chinese were rightly concerned. Only when they perceived that the balance had been righted did they feel more secure in moving toward their "nonaligned" stance.

Certain facts regarding the present status of Sino-Soviet relations are incontrovertible. Economic relations, especially trade, have advanced rapidly from a low base, as noted earlier, and cultural relations have also shown substantial progress. Once again, Chinese citizens are studying in the Soviet Union, and Russian researchers are traveling in China. Russian ballet and motion pictures have made their appearance again in the PRC, and conferences on Russian literature have been held. Chinese acrobats perform in the Soviet Union while Chinese economists explore current trends in the USSR and Eastern Europe. These developments have been accompanied by progresssively higher-level official visits and regularized negotiation sessions.

Meanwhile, there have been some changes in official propaganda on both sides. While criticisms have by no means ceased, forebearance or even complimentary remarks can be discovered in some instances. Chinese assessments of Chernenko at the time of his death, for example, were positive, and Gorbachev has generally been given the benefit of the doubt as his policies are awaited. In exchange, public Soviet attacks on Deng have ceased despite the continuance of private doubts. Of greater importance, the Chinese have acknowledged once again that the USSR is a socialist state, dropping the charge that Russian leadership had led that nation to fascism. In exchange, Moscow also defines the PRC as a socialist nation and now goes to some lengths to endorse the right of each socialist state to find its own road to communism.

Although Chinese leaders may insist that the normalization of Sino-Soviet relations cannot take place until progress has been made in resolving the three obstacles, in most respects normalization is occurring. Even with regard to the three obstacles, the Chinese have modified their position. In addition to removing the insistence that progress in their resolution constituted a precondition for official negotiations, the Chinese have made it clear that the most important obstacle is that of Vietnam. They have even hinted that if the Soviets could persuade the Vietnamese to withdraw from Cambodia, Soviet bases in Vietnam might be tolerated.

Gorbachev's Vladivostok speech of mid-1986 in turn provided the first concrete indication of a Soviet desire to show flexibility on security issues of vital concern to the Chinese without compromising fundamental Soviet interests. The assertion that discussions with the Mongols were taking place, looking toward Soviet troop reduction in the People's Republic of Mongolia, and that the USSR was prepared to undertake broader talks pertaining to a proportionate reduction of land forces by the Soviet Union and China, spoke to one obstacle—long recognized as the easiest with which to deal. On the two other contentious security issues, the Soviet General Secretary was more cautious. A very modest troop reduction in Afghanistan was announced, but Gorbachev reiterated that a political solution here would have to include acceptance of the Soviet-sponsored Kabul government. Regarding Indochina, the item of greatest importance to Beijing, the Russian leader rested with an assertion of Soviet interest in the normalization of Sino-Vietnamese relations while indicating that the clock in Cambodia could not be turned back. In addition to his specific proposals, Gorbachev repackaged the long-standing Soviet advocacy of a conference on Asian Collective Security by advancing the idea of a Helsinki-type conference for all Pacific-Asian nations.

Gorbachev's Vladivostok speech signifies the centrality with which Moscow views its relations with China within the Asian context. It also represents the first signs of a Soviet willingness to move publicly from generalities to specific proposals. Asian governments have long complained about past Soviet negotiating behavior in this respect. The speech must be viewed, moreover, as the opening step in a process which the Russian leaders hope will lead to a new Soviet image in Asia while at the same time advancing Soviet involvements, economically and politically. But what was said—and unsaid—at Vladivostok also highlights the key Soviet dilemma. While showing new flexibility, the Soviet leaders do not want to jeopardize any of their recent political-military gains in Asia or their overall strategic position.

Perhaps it is not surprising that a number of Soviet specialists and government officials voice optimism about the future of Sino-Soviet relations, at least in private conversations. They note that very considerable progress has been made in those relations without the necessity on the Soviet side of making basic strategic concessions, and they believe that with approaches like that of the Vladivostok speech, such progress can continue. China does not fear a Soviet attack, they assert, and the so-called three obstacles will be resolved or reduced with the passage of time. In any case, the obstacles will not stand in the way, assert Soviet specialists, when China's leaders determine that it is in their interest have improved relations with the USSR and aligned states.

Further, as indicated earlier, they argue that after experimentation China will remain in the socialist mainstream. Hence, it will retain a fundamental ideological-political compatability with the Soviet Union. Whether this is an accurate assessment or not, one important fact should be underlined: internal developments in both the PRC and the USSR will have a significant, possibly decisive influence on Sino-Soviet relations. Should the Soviet Union, for instance, follow China in undertaking structural economic reforms, in the process of opening the USSR more fully to market forces and participating increasingly in the international arena, Sino-Soviet political communication—and economic intercourse—would benefit. A similar result might occur if both societies pursued traditional Stalinist policies. But if China continues its reformist course and Soviet leaders merely seek to make the old system work better, interaction of all types will be rendered more difficult.

Soviet spokesmen admit that there will be no return to the conditions of the early 1950s, and some profess to accept this fact with relief, asserting that some embraces can be too tight. More importantly, two concerns manifest themselves in the Soviet analysis of China and its future. One, shared by many other foreign observers, is the question of whether political stability can be maintained in the post-Deng era, and precisely what political-economic course the new leaders will take. It is in the nature of Soviet hopes that the present course will be altered to provide greater opportunities for Sino-Soviet ideological and political compatibility. Thus, many Soviet specialists have underlined the dark aspects of recent developments in China, highlighting the errors and excesses. But attitudes could change if Gorbachev himself were to pursue reforms of similar depth and scope.

Beyond this, however, many Soviets look to the longer-range future with a certain foreboding. There has long been an emotional fear of "the yellow peril" among the broad mass of Russian people. Grassroots Russian prejudice against Chinese has a lengthy history, stretching into czarist times, and it has not disappeared. A reverse current of similar nature runs in China. The depth of xenophobia there has only occasionally been plumbed, most recently during the Cultural Revolution. For the Chinese masses, all foreigners—especially long-nosed ones -are suspect, and that includes the Russians. Sentiments may be different among the most highly educated classes of both societies, but even at this level prejudices lurk.

For many Russians, elites as well as common citizens, moreover, it is difficult to separate the problem of China from the problem of empire.

From Moscow is governed a vast territory encompassing major portions of central and northern Asia, lands harboring diverse Asian peoples whose cultures vary greatly from that of the Greater Russians. Much of this territory was acquired or consolidated only in the nineteenth century. Although Chinese leaders have not recently indicated that they intend to reopen the issue of the legitimacy of Russian rule in Asia, Mao Zedong himself once told Japanese visitors that the Chinese bill for Siberia had not yet been presented to Moscow. Will an economically strong, militarily powerful China present such a bill at some point in the twenty-first century? Or more likely, will Beijing exert growing pressure on the small Asian allies of the USSR in an effort to create a more meaningful buffer zone while also extending its economic reach?

Given recent trends in Sino-Soviet relations, it is interesting to find that the Russians in general are publicly cautious and privately encouraged whereas the Chinese are publicly hopeful and privately pessimistic. In all of this, there may be a considerable element of theater. Views also vary in accordance with the circumstances and the individual. Can the outside observer achieve an objective appraisal of likely future prospects?

Two considerations are uppermost in the minds of Chinese policymakers today: development and security. As suggested, the Soviet contribution to Chinese development, while not apt to be negligible, will fall well below that of Japan and the West unless conditions change radically. Current Chinese leaders look primarily to the latter sources for ideas, training and advanced technology. The security factor will be discussed more fully in the next section. Suffice it to say here that there is little probability of a greatly reduced Soviet military presence in the Pacific-Asia region, and future Chinese leaders are as likely as those of the present to see this as either a constraint or a threat.

In the light of these facts, it is improbable that a broad ideological and systemic similarity between these two states will be sufficient to knit them together politically. On the contrary, despite the homage paid to Marxist-Leninist internationalism, both the USSR and the PRC are certain to continue their pursuit of foreign policies consonant with the practices of the traditional nation-state. Hence, on a wide range of issues, especially those where competition for influence exists, such as Korea and Indochina, deep and abiding political differences seem destined to remain. Within the restraints imposed by these considerations, to be sure, fluctuations toward and away from closer relations will take place, and leadership together with policies on both sides can make some difference. Nevertheless, the basic limits to Pan-Asianism noted earlier will be even more pronounced with respect to Sino-Soviet relations.

Sino-American Relations in Political Perspective

Is the course of Sino-American relations in the political realm likely to develop in a similar fashion? Again, it is well to consider how Sino-American relations are affected by the two themes basic to Chinese policy—development and security. Despite the economic problems explored earlier, Chinese leaders—and a great majority of the techno-crats who work under them—expect far more from the United States than from the Soviet Union in connection with their modernization drive, whether the measurement be trade, training, technology trans-fer or investment. The fact that the United States poses no security threat to China is of at least equal importance, and it explains why Chinese leaders are still prepared to seek a low-level security relation-ship with Washington despite an insistence that their policy is one of nonalignment.

Could this situation change? There are economic developments such as a high level of protectionism, a major depression, or the failure of the Chinese economic reforms that could alter the picture. If a sig-nificant percentage of the Chinese studying in the United States were to refuse to return home, that too could cause a reconsideration of cer-tain policies. On the security front, the Taiwan questions presents the greatest uncertainties. If political developments on Taiwan were to result in either widespread violence and upheaval or a proclamation of Taiwanese independence, PRC leaders might be strongly tempted to intervene. In that event, relations would be deeply troubled not only with the United States, but also with Japan and a number of other Asian states.

On balance, however, economic and security factors sustain rather than threaten the PRC-U.S. relationship. On political issues pertain-ing to Asia other than Taiwan, moreover, there is a wide measure of agreement between the two nations. Both are anxious to see peace maintained on the Korean peninsula. And despite its expression of total fidelity to the basic views of North Korea, China has increasingly pursued a two-Korea policy. This is most evident in the economic realm. PRC-ROK trade has grown dramatically, some of it going directly from Chinese to South Korean ports. Korean firms are now involved in joint ventures in China in barely concealed fashion. Cul-tural exchange has also expanded. Chinese Koreans have been allowed to visit relatives in South Korea, and more recently, South Koreans have been permitted to go to Northeast China for similar pur-poses. Chinese and South Korean scholars now meet regularly in third countries and at international conferences. Negotiations of a quasi-official nature, moreover, have been conducted on such matters as hijackings.

Publicly and privately, and with varying degrees of sincerity, PRC authorities insist that the United States should withdraw its troops from South Korea, participate in trilateral negotiations with the North and South, and limit military exercises in the vicinity of the Korean peninsula. They also back Kim Il Sung's proposals for reunification and pay homage to Kim Chong-il as his father's successor. U.S. authorities are prepared to accept these assertions with minimal protest since they are regarded as the price to be paid by China for keeping North Korean authorities from openly criticizing Beijing. It is widely recognized that Pyongyang is unhappy both with the PRC flirtation with South Korea and with its measure of accord with the United States.

For several years, the Chinese effort has been to show Pyongyang the benefits of PRC economic reforms, including that of turning outward for science and technology. Beijing has used the argument that North-South negotiations would smooth the path to broadened relations between North Korea and Japan, and with the United States as well. Not incidentally, such developments would also make China's own two-Korea policy easier to sustain. Hence, Beijing has taken an active role as middleman between North Korea and the two advanced industrial states. Thus far, its efforts have had limited success. Yet North-South dialogues continue sporadically, Japan shows signs of a willingness to modestly upgrade its relations with the North, and the United States has permitted cultural contacts with Pyongyang. The basic compatibility of the Korean policies of the PRC and the United States, however, lies in the fact that both insist that reunification must be peaceful, and both pursue policies that acknowledge the existence of two Korean states.

Southeast Asia, once the source of major contention between China and the United States, currently presents few problems. China has largely abandoned its support for guerilla Communist movements in the region, at least for the present, and in its foreign policies places the premium upon state-to-state relations. In particular, its cultivation of the states belonging to ASEAN accords with American policies. Similarly, its staunch opposition to Vietnam's efforts to dominate Cambodia and Laos creates no problem for the United States, although a coordination of ASEAN and Chinese policies has placed the United States in an awkward position on occasion. In general, however, there are no major political issues separating Washington and Beijing in this region. China does have territorial claims in the South China Sea that might cause future problems, and the large Chinese ethnic communities in the region always pose a potential difficulty, especially should China seek greater influence within Southeast Asia. But for the present, the joint concerns of the United States and China are principally with Soviet and Vietnamese expansion.

In South Asia, also, there is a strong measure of accord. Both China and the United States condemn Soviet intervention in Afghanistan and provide assistance to the mujahedeen. Both have hoped for improvements in relations with the Rajiv Gandhi administration in India, but neither is prepared to pay for such improvements by downgrading relations with Pakistan. Both seek good relations with the small states of South Asia, risking the disapproval of New Delhi, which is not prepared to share power with another major state in the region, at least apart from the USSR.

The strong measure of political agreement between China and the United States with regard to East and South Asia, however, does not extend to most other areas. Beijing's criticism of American policies in the so-called Third World has been unremittingly harsh, as has been its view of many of the Reagan administration's domestic programs. One senses that top party and government authorities in China are anxious to portray the United States to their citizenry in a negative light partly to dampen an enthusiasm for this open, affluent society that might otherwise get out of hand. Indeed, the campaign against "spiritual pollution" has had as one of its main targets liberalism and "the decadent culture" of the West. We are witnessing yet another episode in the historic effort of Chinese leaders to borrow Western technology but retain indigenous values, an effort no more likely to succeed today than in the past, at least in any full measure. Indeed, recently, Chinese leaders themselves have signaled the need for far-reaching political reforms to accompany and bolster economic changes. We may witness significant political changes in China in the near future in the direction of greater openness. In the long term, if the past is any guide, one may expect surges of relative openness and extensive borrowing, cultural as well as technological, to be followed by retrenchments involving the denunciation of excessive foreignism and reassertions of Chinese values—now a mixture of Sinicized Marxism and more traditional beliefs.

In response to recent Chinese attacks, certain Americans have strongly protested Beijing's treatment of U.S. policies and the PRC voting record in the United Nations, warning that China cannot expect to be given economic and strategic treatment as a friend if it behaves as an opponent. The Chinese have not taken such criticism very seriously, blandly responding that their duty and right lie in attacking erroneous or immoral policies, whoever is responsible. But they also assert that nonalignment does not mean equidistance between the United States and the Soviet Union. They proclaim privately that they see the Soviet Union as China's primary enemy. In reality, China's current policy is one of tilted nonalignment, and the tilt is perceptibly toward Japan and the United States. There is always the risk for China that a trend toward maximum accommodation with Russia, private assurances notwithstanding, or sustained, caustic criticisms of the United States will erode American confidence in China's future course and create growing doubts as to the compatibility of the two states. At present, however, common interests—and mutual apprehensions of the USSR—override differences and sustain a relationship that is still expanding, and that could have a decisive influence on the entire Pacific-Asian area.

The United States and the Soviet Union in Northeast Asia

It remains to examine the political relations between the United States and the Soviet Union as they pertain to Northeast Asia, and then to explore the relative position of the two superpowers in their competition for influence within the region as a whole. Since American-Soviet relations are intrinsically global in nature, it is axiomatic that no area can be viewed as a separate theater of superpower operations. Certain general principles should thus be established, applicable not only to Northeast Asia but to other regions as well.

First, when U.S.-USSR relations are minimal and hostile, as in recent years, cooperation on regional issues is correspondingly reduced.

Second, even under these conditions, certain understandings prevail, often unstated. For example, neither state wants a regional crisis to lead to nuclear conflict. Hence, when one of the two superpowers seeks to expand its influence or becomes extensively involved in a given state or region, it is forced to tolerate counterintervention by the other power, directly or through surrogates.

Third, both superpowers have shown a degree of uncertainty about how to connect the central issue of arms control with a range of political issues from human rights to acts of intervention in foreign states. Direct linkage, sometimes attempted by the United States and more recently threatened by the USSR, has not served the purpose intended, namely, to force a retreat from the action being undertaken. Hence, it is likely to be set aside in favor of parallelism, the enumeration of grievances with a demand for remedial action in conjunction with arms control negotiations, but without the stipulation that a solution of these issues is a prerequisite for arms control agreements. In this manner, both parties can seek to cultivate a political atmosphere at home and abroad conducive to strengthening their general bargaining position without bringing negotiations on the central issue to a halt. In this connection, the Soviet commitment to competition with the United States in the political arena has been considerably heightened with the advent of Gorbachev.

Fourth, in recent times, the Soviet Union has insisted upon being treated as a global power, one not to be ignored in any region of the world. In Asia, it has underscored this demand by first expanding its military power, then seeking to add economic and political components to strengthen that power, in the process extending its reach to areas previously neglected.

Fifth, Soviet psychology as revealed in foreign policy is reflected in a complex admixture of defensiveness and aggressive behavior, feelings of inferiority and a desire to be respected, yet a bruskness and insensitivity in dealing with others.

American psychology in its international manifestations is also complex. A desire to be loved vies with a desire to be respected similar to that of the Russians. Moral imperatives regarding American policy contest with the requirements of exercising power. U.S. interventionist acts evoke sharp feelings of guilt or desires for withdrawal to cut costs and risks on the part of a sizable, often growing segment of the American public. Hamlet's agonies are constantly replicated.

Using these general principles as the context, the relative political standing of the USSR and the United States may be compared in the two other major states of Northeast Asia and in the region as a whole. It is appropriate to commence with Japan, the nation so central to all others in this area. Here, the Soviets can scarcely be happy with their position. Whatever the hopes for improvement contained in the most recent developments, Soviet status in Japan is abysmally low. In company with some others, Russian's operating principle has been that the Japanese respond only to harsh treatment. Thus, whether the issue has been Japanese prisoners of war, the emperor, reparations, territorial jurisdiction, or economic negotiations, the Soviet position has been unremittingly tough for more than forty years.

The results have been as one might expect. The USSR has virtually no political constituency in Japan. Even the Japan Communist Party has distanced itself from Moscow, associating its position with that of the Communist Party of China in an earlier period, but in recent years adopting an independent stance and generally aligning its philosophic views with West European Communists like the Italians. Only elements from the "left faction" of the Japan Socialist Party and groups having a special economic interest in the USSR have shown any affinity for Moscow. The mainstream of the JSP under Ishibashi Masashi sought to establish normal relations with the USSR, meeting with Gorbachev and transmitting the contents of his conversation to

Nakasone. But Ishibashi's objective was a Japanese position of rough equidistance among China, the USSR and the United States. His successor will presumably follow a similar course. The Socialists are also moving to establish contact with South Korea as a complement to their long-standing ties with the North. Thus, the overture to the Soviet Union comes from a neutralist commitment, not one of alignment.

Even distiguished Soviet specialists on Japan are divided over the prospects for the future. Some, especially of an older generation, continue to be exponents of the tough line and are prepared to assume that the chemistry between Russians and Japanese will always be bad. At certain earlier points, however, sporadic Soviet efforts were made to extend a small olive branch. Some Russians indicated that although they accepted the primacy of the American-Japanese relationship, improvements in relations between the Soviet Union and Japan would not threaten that alliance. As noted, the opportunities afforded by Siberia have been held out periodically to interested Japanese parties, and a few joint projects have been undertaken. Fishery agreements, moreover, constitute a perennial card for the Soviets. Beyond strictly economic ties, unofficial bilateral meetings of specialists have been held to discuss contemporary issues. Yet neither singly nor collectively have these activities resulted in basic improvements in Soviet-Japanese ties. Generally, they have served merely to reveal the depth of the mistrust.

In the recent past, as suggested earlier, the Soviet Union under Gorbachev has signaled an interest in improving relations with Japan as a part of its broader effort to refurbish and strengthen its position in East Asia. First, discussions have been initiated at high levels, through the visits of principal Asian dignitaries to Moscow and of key Soviet figures to Asia. Invitations to visit Moscow have been tendered to oppositionists as well as those in power, particularly when they have been deemed susceptible to Soviet views. Second, proposals for cooperation in both economic and cultural fields have been advanced, with the pledge to follow up general discussions with the exploration of concrete projects, including specific trade agreements, technology arrangements, student exchanges and artistic performances. Third, in the past, proposals for bilateral or multilateral agreements on broad principles were put on the table without any previous settlement of those specific strategic and political issues of paramount importance to the contracting parties. Understandably, this approach met with strong disapproval from the Asian states. The Gorbachev initiative now seeks to alter that strategy, indicating a Soviet willingness to deal with concrete grievances and problems in company with a movement toward more general accord.

In the final analysis, however, the success of the current Soviet

41

approach to Asia is likely to hinge on whether Moscow is prepared to make basic changes in political-strategic policies while at the same time expanding its economic relations on a substantial scale. As yet, there is little evidence to suggest that USSR leaders are able to take such a course rapidly, given the circumstances in which they find themselves. At the same time, both personnel changes and recent pronouncements indicate that all feasible alternatives are being explored in Moscow in an effort to break away from the frozen past. In sum, East Asia is being given much higher priority on the Soviet agenda.

As suggested, the above conditions apply to the Soviet approaches being made to China and the ASEAN bloc as well as to Japan. Opinion within the PRC varies as to how seriously to take Gorbachev's recent overtures, and how far the Soviet Union may be prepared to go in modifying past positions. The old stance that China had to negotiate with Mongolia concerning Soviet troop withdrawal from that country has been altered, but China is still supposed to deal with Vietnam regarding Cambodia and with the Kabul government regarding Afghanistan, albeit with the possibility of Soviet activity behind the scenes.

Most Beijing leaders remain skeptical. Yet, as indicated earlier, the Russian leaders have some reason to be satisfied. In the 1970s, the Soviet Union saw the United States steadily improving its relations with both Beijing and Moscow while Sino-Soviet relations remained mired in hostility. At the beginning of the 1980s, however, in response to overtures from Brezhnev and others, China initiated an offer to reopen a dialogue with Moscow, setting aside the ban on talks that followed the Afghanistan invasion. The agreements reached, moreover, have been at no cost to the USSR, and the PRC threat to withhold "normalization" unless Soviet basic strategic concessions are forthcoming carries increasingly less weight. Meanwhile, a new Soviet initiative has been launched which at a minimum has cosmetic value and, over time, may offer more. Russian leaders are well aware of the major change that has taken place in Chinese foreign policy, and the reasons therefore. They now have less reason to fear a Sino-American strategic alliance against them, and they can envisage the possibility that either developments internal to China or some issue such as Taiwan might upset the still fragile Sino-American relationship.

It is for these reasons that Soviet leaders are cautiously optimistic about their position vis-à-vis that of the United States with respect to China, at least in the short to medium term. Nevertheless, as indicated, fundamental geopolitical, cultural, nationalist and developmental factors combine to preclude a close Sino-Soviet relationship, and the Russians cannot rid themselves of a deep foreboding about

China's power and potential role in the twenty-first century.

The current status of USSR-U.S. relations is also reflected in the political position and policies of the Soviet Union toward the smaller societies of Northeast Asia. Moscow has long held reservations with respect to North Korea and its paramount leader, Kim Il Sung. Privately, the Soviets have regarded North Koreans as aloof to the point of rudeness, ungrateful for past Russian assistance, and prone to a pro-China tilt. Kim himself is seen as a megalomaniac whose cult of personality has little in common with Marxism-Leninism. The North Koreans including Kim have corresponding private criticisms of the Russians: heavy-handedness and a chauvinistic attitude in dealing with allies; limited generosity in dispensing assistance; and a low culture.

Despite these mutual misgivings, however, the USSR has aimed at improving its relations with North Korea in recent times, strictly from a calculation of national interests, taking into account the challenges and opportunities derivative from the policies of the United States and the PRC. The overtures to Pyongyang began at the end of the 1970s, with higher-level visits, more favorable propaganda, and increased involvement in the North Korean effort to modernize its industries. Initially, these activities had limited success, and the Soviets continued to be reluctant to provide modern military technology or extensive economic aid. More recently, however, several factors have motivated the Russians to increase aid and establish closer ties. Moscow has grown increasingly concerned about what it labels a strategic entente among the United States, Japan and South Korea—a development regarded as a further projection of American power against the vulnerable Soviet Far East. In addition, the Soviet Union does not want to be odd man out on the Korean peninsula, a stance in keeping with its insistence upon being treated as a global power. For example, Soviet spokesmen have taken a very reserved view of trilateral discussions that would involve only the United States and the two Koreas, despite the ardent support of such talks by both Pyongyang and Beijing.

Thus, the Soviets have made available MIG 23s and other military equipment to North Korea. They have pledged additional assistance in the upgrading of plants and facilities. Soviet North Korean trade has long constituted a critical element in the DPRK economy, and in recent years it has represented one-third or more of the total North Korean trade, a vastly larger amount than with China. In seeking to overcome the problems of autarky, the North Koreans are more than ever dependent upon the USSR and East Europe. In addition, the Russians have continuously expanded high-level visits with the North Koreans, Kim Il Sung going to Moscow, Alieyev and Shevardnadze visiting Pyongyang. And, most significantly, the Soviets have finally acknowledged Kim Chong-il as the heir apparent, thereby fulfilling one of the elder Kim's most insistent requirements.

For all of these benefits, Pyongyang must pay a price. North Korea now permits Soviet overflights and port visits. The overflights allow Soviet aircraft to conduct surveillance far down the China coast, and port visits by Russian naval vessels could bring Soviet warships onto the west side of the Korean peninsula, very close to some of China's vital industrial regions. The North Koreans have long recognized the Kamal government in Afghanistan. More recently, they have upgraded their representation in Hanoi, sending back an ambassador—although out of deference to Prince Sihanouk, Kim Il Sung's friend, Pyongyang refrains from giving Vietnam support for its operations in Cambodia. In general, however, North Korea has edged closer to the Soviet position on various fronts, and this is displayed in its propaganda, which is noticeably more friendly to the USSR than has been the case in many years.

Do these developments disturb China, and thereby create a real or potential threat to the recent improvements in Sino-Soviet relations? Officially, the Chinese insist that they are not concerned. The improvement in relations with the Soviet Union, they assert, makes it possible for North Korea to have good relations with both major states. They add that the DPRK will never abandon its devotion to *chuch'e* (self-reliance) to become a Soviet satellite, and they exhibit confidence that China's greater understanding of Korean culture will always sustain Sino-North Korean relations. Yet from some Chinese quarters, one hears that the larger Soviet military presence in or over North Korea is not comforting. Nor can there be any doubt that China continues to regard Korea as its legitimate sphere of influence. The issues here are delicate ones for all three Communist states.

If Soviet-North Korean relations have noticeably improved, those with South Korea have remained at a low level. This situation also reflects recent trends in U.S.-USSR relations. Earlier, when Soviet relations with the United States were relatively smooth, Moscow showed an interest in cultivating unofficial ties with the South, especially during periods of intense irritation at Pyongyang. Soviet and South Korean representatives met at international sports meets, conferences, and on a more intimate basis in third countries. Such contacts were facilitated because Soviet citizens of Korean ancestry have an almost uniform aversion to the North Korean government, and some had earlier been ousted from the DPRK where they had served as high-ranking officials. Privately, certain Soviet Asian specialists were prepared to talk about how the ties with South Korea might be strengthened, although there was no thought of formal diplomatic relations, given the reluctance to alienate the North completely. But as U.S.-USSR relations soured, and incidents like the KAL tragedy erupted, Soviet interest in improving relations with Seoul waned. USSR propaganda denouncing the Chun Doo Hwan government became virtually indistinguishable from that of Pyongyang. Unlike Beijing, Moscow is not following a two-Korea policy at this time, but it too wants peace maintained on the Korean peninsula since the risks entailed in a conflict there would be very grave.

Toward Taiwan, the Soviets maintain a hands-off policy, There was a time when the USSR seemed tempted to twist the dragon's tail by flirting with Taiwan, but this was when Sino-Soviet relations were at low ebb. Soviet leaders are too wise not to recognize that Taiwan is an issue best left to Americans. It is very unlikely that they would add yet a fourth obstacle to the improvement of Sino-Soviet relations, even if the authorities on Taiwan were interested, which is currently not the case.

The longest and most solid alliance existing between the USSR and an Asian state is that with the People's Republic of Mongolia. The present state of Mongolia was created by Bolshevik power in 1921, and it has been maintained by Soviet power in the ensuing decades. The choices available to Mongolia in international relations are limited. A land large in area and small in population (less than two million), it must be dependent on either China or Russia. For centuries, it was a part of the Manchu-led Chinese empire, and the fear that China might again seek control over their country runs very deeply in the Mongolian mind. The Mongol leaders of the MPR cannot forget that there are more Mongols in the PRC than in the MPR, compatriots who in their eyes are being forcibly Sinicized. Thus, the Soviet Union is identified as protector, at least by those in power, and its military, economic and political presence is exceedingly strong, although it is easy to identify the continued existence of Mongolian culture and a fierce determination on the part of Mongol spokesmen to proclaim their identity as an independent nation.

Once again, the shadow of major power relations falls heavily upon this land. In the era of Sino-Soviet friendship, thousands of Chinese workers toiled in Mongolia, providing labor for various projects. Later, these workers were to be ousted as tension between the USSR and the PRC mounted and the Mongolian border, like that between Soviet and Chinese territory, became a heavily militarized zone, with tens of thousands of Soviet troops and a full range of modern military equipment. With the Sino-Soviet thaw and indications of the withdrawal of some Soviet troops, relations between the MPR and the PRC may improve, but given past history, the two states are not likely to become intimate.

At an earlier point, the United States had the opportunity to open diplomatic relations with the MPR, but it decided not to take this step in deference to the Chiang Kai-shek administration in Taiwan. Later, when negotiations were reopened, last-minute obstacles came from the Mongolian side, in a period of multiple problems between the United States and the USSR, including Vietnam. Now, once again, there are indications that the times may be propitious for new U.S.-MPR discussions on the establishment of cultural relations and diplomatic ties, but the tempo and extent of such developments may depend upon trends in Soviet-American relations. Ironically, Japan, the wartime enemy, has diplomatic relations with Mongolia, in addition to modest economic and cultural ties. Clearly, the Mongols would benefit from relations with all of the major powers.

In summary, the political position of the Soviet Union in Northeast Asia remains weak notwithstanding the gains of the recent past. Despite—or perhaps because of—its growing military strength in the area, the USSR is less well situated politically than was the case thirty-five years ago when its alliance with China seemed firm, North Korea was a client state, and Japan scarcely counted. Behind this fact lie complex problems that remain to be resolved. With few exceptions, its Asian neighbors have found the Soviet Union overbearing. Beyond this, neither the Soviet political structure nor its economic system serves as a model at this point in history. On the contrary, although each of the Asian Communist states bears the pervasive legacy of earlier Soviet influence, all in their own way are in the process of exploring new routes, modifying older structures that are no longer serviceable. Indeed, the USSR itself is a part of that process. And everywhere, Marxism-Leninism has become dogma, having increasingly less intellectual or emotional appeal. For better or worse, nationalism is the dominant political force. The vision of a community of socialist states faded in the 1960s, and it will not return. The Leninist states now operate in the orthodox fashion of nations everywhere, with perceived national interests the true determinants of policy.

What are the concrete implications of the fact that the Soviet Union comes to Asia today without its earlier political advantages? The opportunity to lead or influence the anti-imperialist movement has been greatly diminished, with the Soviet Union itself frequently on the defensive against charges of big-power chauvinism. Socialist idealism has been replaced by the search for workable programs, and an international socialist community under Soviet guidance no longer attracts adherents. The USSR must now make its way in Asia—and in the world at large—as another nation-state, militarily powerful but in most other respects only part of the way down the road to modernization, belonging in many senses to the great body of "developing nations," hence forced to learn more than to teach.

Let us now turn to the other superpower. Are the political tides in Asia flowing in such a fashion as to enhance the influence of the United States? The picture is a mixed one. As noted, the basic political rapport between the United States and Japan has been a source of strength, enabling both nations to cope better with the serious economic problems between them. To be sure, these problems have been turned into political issues in the legislatures of the two countries, especially the United States. Nevertheless, the political strength of the American-Japanese alliance has bolstered the relationship in a time of stress.

With China, the commonality of interests lies primarily in the strategic rather than the political realm. Americans scan the horizon to see whether a fifth modernization, that of political freedom, will be added to the other four. If they are discerning, observers can see a zigzag pattern, as on the economic front, but with authoritarianism the predominant mode, party dictatorship the instrument, and intellectual conformity the safest course. Yet because not more is expected, because Chinese dissidents do not have a large constituency in the United States, and because the unique problems of modernizing this vast society are appreciated, the human rights issue is raised in the United States only peripherally with respect to China in contrast to the heat generated over this issue as it applies to authoritarian-pluralist societies like South Korea or Taiwan.

The role of human rights in U.S. foreign policy is destined never to be resolved in a manner that will satisfy all Americans—or those governments with which the United States is associated. In the eyes of many U.S. citizens, support for governments that restrict civil rights and pursue authoritarian policies is both immoral and, in the long run, self-defeating since the citizenry of the government being supported may turn against the United States. Why should sacrifices of treasure and even blood be undertaken, the critics ask, if those supported act in ways contrary to American values.

Yet these simple—and to some, incontrovertible—axioms, if applied rigorously, could lead to disaster, both in strategic terms and in terms of the very values the United States is seeking to promote. Even the Carter administration, as strongly committed to human rights as it was, discovered that other factors had to be considered in making foreign policy, and also that a black and white delineation of societies on the basis of their being "free" or "unfree" was naive.

The number of American- or Western-style democracies in the world is small, and there is no indication that the democratic ranks (as Americans would define that category) will rapidly swell in the immediate future. There are a number of authoritarian-pluralist societies in

Asia in the process of trying to make the very difficult transition toward competitive politics and the expansion of civil rights. The factors that shape the success or failure of such efforts are many and complex—among them, the traditions of the society, the training and values of current elites, the socioeconomic setting, the external environment, and the political behavior of the principal factions. As suggested, rarely does the political trend move in a single direction; reverses are not uncommon. Nor can one predict the future of democracy in Asia or elsewhere with any certainty, although some developments are promising.

In this context, two points are germane. First, it is essential to make distinctions between those societies where socioeconomic pluralism operates in such a manner as to support political evolution, and those societies where statism is so powerful as to preclude or make exceedingly difficult peaceful evolution. In general, authoritarian-pluralist societies fall into the first category; most if not all Leninist societies are to be found in the second category. Indeed, the instability that prevails in many authoritarian-pluralist societies today is precisely because an evolution is under way, with heightened tension between a still strongly traditional polity and a dynamic socioeconomic revolution. Instability, if it surfaces at all in a Leninist society, is generally smashed in a ruthless fashion or forced to pursue a subversive course. Those individuals who cannot recognize this difference as in the case of North and South Korea, for example, can do the cause of democracy no good.

A second matter of importance is interrelated. What form of intervention on behalf of human rights on the part of a powerful nation like the United States is likely to have the greatest effect in the direction desired? This issue is especially acute where the U.S. capacity to deal a damaging blow to the government in power is substantial, as is the case with many of the smaller nations heavily dependent upon American support. Human rights attacks upon states like the USSR or the PRC may or may not produce results (generally, frontal, public assaults garner only counterblasts about interference in the domestic affairs of a sovereign nation and produce negative or marginal results). In any case, they do not threaten the government in power. That is not necessarily the case with some of the authoritarian-pluralist states closely aligned with the United States. Here, American leverage against those in power is much greater. But the open and heavy-handed use of such leverage entails risks. Such intervention lays any government using it open to charges of imperialism, and if it is based on a faulty premise—namely, an assumption that a given society can fully operate democratic institutions when that is not the case—then the United States may be committed to steadily deepening involvement in the politics of another society without a reasonable chance of success.

Some forms of U.S. pressure can be effective with authoritarian allies. Generally, they are the more discreet pressures, wielded from behind the scenes so that they do not involve the type of direct confrontation that causes an irreparable loss of face, and hence the likelihood of a stiffening resistance under nationalist banners. Governments dependent in some degree upon U.S. aid and protection must be caused to recognize that the American people and Congress will not easily countenance sacrifices for causes in which they do not believe or on behalf of leaders concerning whose values and capacities they have grave doubts, unless the security of the United States itself is directly involved. The latter situation produced the U.S.-USSR alignment during World War II.

But how does one judge progress with respect to human rights? What is the balance sheet at this writing on leaders like Chiang Ching-kuo, Chun Doo Hwan, Deng Xiaoping, Kim Il Sung and the governments that they head? The tabulation in most cases will be complex, but any fair inquiry will reveal that Chiang and Chun, whatever their political reservations and regressions, have committed themselves to processes involving a widening arena for political expression, competitive elections, and a willingness to tolerate an open opposition. These commitments are less clear in the case of Deng and his supporters despite the pledge of "socialist legalism," certain gains for political rights since 1978, and the recent official support for political reform. We will watch political developments in China with great interest. With respect to Kim Il Sung, no political evolution whatsoever can be discerned.

Prior to comparing U.S. policies toward the small states of Northeast Asia with those of the USSR, one final observation is in order. As signaled earlier, the United States stands virtually alone among the major powers in making political values a significant element in its foreign policy. In earlier times, both the Soviet Union and China made ideological purity (agreement) a cardinal issue on occasion, but behind this effort to elevate values to a supreme position lay an attempt to enforce obedience to external authority. Abstract moral commitments were strictly secondary. In any case, this approach has been largely set aside. Neither Moscow nor Beijing is concerned as to whether Kim Il Sung is a good Marxist-Leninist nor, for that matter, whether Gorbachev or Deng Xiaoping deserves that appellation. And as has been indicated, Japanese leaders become uneasy when Washington appears to be making human rights a principal determinant of its policies toward important states.

Nonetheless, the human rights issue has long rendered U.S. political relations with countries like South Korea and Taiwan complex. Neither of these societies is a democracy, despite the expansion of political rights and participation. When there is a reversion to repression, it frequently produces a sharp American reaction. On occasion, this has been conducive to changes of policy or personnel on the part of the government challenged. But the fundamental political course has answered more to a combination of indigenous socioeconomic developments and external security threats.

At present, the United States watches anxiously as the ROK tries to change a government born of a military coup to a government based upon open, competitive elections. There are clearly hazards. Sizable portions of the Korean elite, in and out of power, have a limited tolerance for any opposition and a limited ability to compromise. Moreover, the political spectrum at both ends stretches beyond the type of consensus on political means and ends required for the effective operation of democratic institutions. It will be essential to build or shore up all available centrist elements if democracy is to work. Currently, one political issue of importance is whether the president should be elected by the citizenry directly or through the system of electors as provided in the present constitution. A more fundamental issue being debated is whether a parliamentary system might serve the needs of the society better than a presidential system. These debates take place in the streets as well as in the national assembly. Meanwhile, Korea prepares for the Olympics and national elections, both scheduled for 1988. These events—and particularly the former one—produce great unhappiness in North Korea, hence, the temptation to cause disruptions. The future may well be difficult.

In this setting, the United States has sought to walk down a narrow, poorly marked path. On the one hand, it has served as a rest and recuperation center for various South Korean opposition figures and, on occasion, intervened sternly if privately with the South Korean government when an affair like the Kim Dae Jung kidnapping occurs. At the same time, it has been unwilling or unable to thwart the military coups which on two occasions brought to power a government by nonconstitutional means and of which it did not initially approve. And it has eventually supported both governments that resulted from these military actions, those of Park Chung Hee and Chun Doo Hwan, in the process averring its continued adherence to defense commitments that now extend nearly forty years.

Meanwhile, Korean nationalism has steadily risen, taking diverse forms. In the militant student movement where dependency theories and other neo-Marxist concepts have enjoyed increasing currency, nationalism takes on an anti-American flavor. But it should not be thought that such a trend comes only from the left. Within government circles and in the business community as well, sensitivities with respect to Korean sovereignty and Korean rights are more acute than at any time since independence—a fitting companion to the emergence of the Republic of Korea as a medium power. Resentment is openly expressed against "American political interference" and American actions to counter alleged unfair trade practices by Korean companies.

While the United States will ignore these developments at its peril, the strong majority of Korean citizens and their government recognize that at this point, the U.S. tie is essential to the survival of the ROK. Even the moderate opposition wants a continued American presence, and many within this group want more, not less American intervention in the Korean political arena *providing* it favors them. Public opinion polls continue to indicate that for a strong majority of the Korean people, the U.S.-ROK relationship is a positive one.

The North poses a different dilemma for the United States. Despite the opprobrium heaped upon the U.S. government and its policies by North Korean spokesmen, the DPRK government has made it clear that not only would it like to engage the United States in a dialogue relating to troop withdrawal from the South, but it is also prepared, indeed anxious, to meet with "individuals of influence" and select others to create a climate for expanded relations. Thus far, the U.S. response has been a cautious one—not necessarily opposed to academic contacts, but not desirous of moving toward the type of dialogue that might seem to confer de facto recognition and could only end in failure because of the nature of DPRK demands. Washington is also aware of ROK qualms about unilateral American action, given the rocky, uncertain road over which North-South relations have traveled in recent years. Slowly, American contacts with North Koreans may expand, but even with respect to informal meetings of a cultural type, U.S. relations with North Korea are likely to hinge on progress in North-South talks, and beyond this, on North Korean actions with respect to the Korean peninsula and elsewhere. The United States has long been on record as favoring cross-recognition (U.S. and Japan recognition of the DPRK in exchange for PRC and USSR recognition of the ROK) and the admission of both Koreas to the United Nations, but Kim Il Sung has thus far vetoed both of those steps. The United States is not likely to entertain any scheme involving unilateral recognition of the North.

Given the commitments of the United States and the USSR with regard to the Korean peninsula, a hard core of mutual interest exists despite the different roads the two powers have followed. Each must worry about political developments that could produce the type of crisis that might result in involving it at a level not desired. What will be

51

the nature of the DPRK in the post-Kim Il Sung era? Can the ROK avoid recurrent instability or major upheaval in the years immediately ahead? Will North-South talks make progress, continue in stalemate, or collapse? Neither the United States nor the USSR wants another Korean war, as indicated earlier, and both have an interest in restraining the Korean state with which they are associated by one of the several means available to them.

In political terms, the United States has certain current advantages despite the precarious nature of the South Korean scene. Its policies have the general support of Japan, and in more limited degree of China, whereas the USSR is largely on its own, operating outside any consultative framework. Despite the rise of anti-Americanism within certain South Korean circles, moreover, the United States has a much larger Korean constituency friendly to it than does the USSR. Even in the North, the Soviets are regarded as a necessary evil by those who cultivate them rather than as a trusted ally.

With respect to Taiwan, on the other hand, the long-term political advantages may rest with the Soviet Union, although that is by no means clear. As indicated earlier, Moscow intends to leave Taiwan as an issue between the United States and the PRC, believing that this unresolved matter could provoke a major confrontation or, at a minimum, provide a continuing irritant. The United States, urged by China to take a more active role in bringing the Taiwan authorities into negotiations with Beijing, has been rightly reluctant to undertake such an assignment. Its efforts would surely be rebuked by the current ROC leaders, who still blame the Truman administration for attempting to build a coalition government in China after 1945, supposedly allowing the Communists time to consolidate and strengthen their position. Beyond this, however, U.S. intervention would reopen the China issue in American politics—something that no one should want. Moreover, the chances of any successful conclusion to formal negotiations now is virtually nil since the Taiwan government is being asked to negotiate its own demise as a sovereign entity.

Meanwhile, Taiwan is one of many societies facing a generational transition, with an older group of mainland refugees giving way to younger leaders, a mixture of second-generation refugees and Taiwanese. Here too, political uncertainties abound, and the chances of recurrent instability are not negligible. Connected with the issue of economic policy and political succession, moreover, is the growing crisis of identity. Forsaken diplomatically by all but a handful of nations, the people of Taiwan increasingly ask, "Who are we?" The old political institutions cannot survive much longer, yet what new ones can provide stability and security along with the values to which a majority of citizens subscribe?

In this setting, the United States continues to be crucial to Taiwan—the government as well as the people—despite the events of the 1970s. U.S.-Taiwan economic relations have never been more extensive. And the Taiwan authorities have assiduously cultivated relations with many states and cities, shrewdly realizing that in the American federal system, it is not just Washington that counts. As a result, the political base of Taiwan in the United States may be as strong as it was before derecognition. Certainly, there is no indication that the Taiwan Relations Act will be repealed.

Whether this will lead to a future U.S.-PRC confrontation cannot now be predicted. If the trend is toward increased economic intercourse and cultural exchanges between China and Taiwan, with the political systems of both societies evolving toward a more relaxed atmosphere, the prospects for a harmonious relationship would be hopeful. It is easy, however, to envisage a less happy scenario, one leading to threats and conflict. In such an event, the whole of Asia would be adversely affected, not least of all, China.

If Taiwan has been in its international dimensions "an American problem," Mongolia might be categorized as "a Soviet problem," since the extensive Soviet commitment to that nation has periodically produced heightened tension between Russia and China. As indicated earlier, the United States may be in a position to establish cultural and diplomatic relations with the People's Republic of Mongolia and, because the circumstances are very different from those that influence Soviet actions regarding Taiwan, it is an alternative that should be reexamined.

When one compares the political position of the United States and the USSR in Northeast Asia, there can be no doubt of American primacy. It is not merely that the USSR has failed to cultivate this aspect of its policies in the region. The more serious problem lies in the fact that the Soviet Union has little to offer the states of Northeast Asia politically. Its ideology and political system were transplanted decades ago to three states of the region and continue to have a deep impact there, but except for Mongolia, Russian expansionism and heavy-handedness in the decades that followed World War II alienated even the governments that adopted Soviet institutions. Thus, Gorbachev must construct a political base for the Soviet Union anew, building a different edifice on the ruins of the old structure.

The United States faces a different set of problems. Political ties with most of the governments of the region range from reasonably good to excellent, Mongolia and North Korea being the exceptions. And the image of the United States among the articulate citizenry of aligned states is as positive as that of any foreign society. However, the standards to which the United States is held are incomparably higher than those applied to the USSR. Moreover, rival elites demand diametrically opposite policies. Governments want support, and an assurance of the continuity of American policies. Oppositionists want protection at a minimum and, optimally, policies that will result in bringing them to power. These conflicting desires, moreover, are promoted in a period when rapid change is endemic throughout the region and the United States wrestles with the problem of creating a balance between the costly, painful role of being an international power and giving greater attention to pressing domestic problems.

Conclusions

Once again, it is time to draw general conclusions from this survey of the politics of Northeast Asia with special reference to the major powers.

First, while the basic ideological-systemic divisions among the states of this region complicate or facilitate relations, alignments and cleavages today cannot be explained by relying primarily upon such divisions. The times bear witness to serious rifts among Leninist societies, problems of growing complexity among democratic states, and alignments that cross ideological barriers. Today, relations between and among states are most likely to be governed by two overriding considerations: security and development. State behavior, moreover, irrespective of the ideological banners flown or the institutional structure implanted, follows the classic nation-state model.

Second, although the politics of Northeast Asia are in great flux, basic systemic changes are likely to be rare. The Leninist, democratic, and authoritarian types will each be represented in the Northeast Asian political firmament for the foreseeable future. Such changes as are occuring, however, point in a general direction: certain authoritarian-pluralist states are moving toward greater political openness, and one Leninist nation, China, is acquiring additional attributes of the authoritarian-pluralist state. If the movement is generally away from the Soviet model, however, the United States no more than the USSR can expect its values or system to be replicated in pure form. One of the many political challenges to the United States is learning to live with this fact.

Third, one can discern political attributes accruing to the soft regionalism that is emerging in Northeast Asia and, on a broader level, a process of Asianization as the network of ties among East Asian states thickens. Pan-Asianism, however, is not going to be the wave of the future. Like the concept of a socialist community, its time has passed, even as an ideal.

Fourth, in Asia as elsewhere, the general trend is from alliance to alignment, and that central fact colors many of the political relationships of the region. Despite rhetoric, nonalignment is invariably part myth—virtually every nation tilts. It is no longer necessary, or indeed possible, for most states to pledge absolute allegiance to the major power with which they are aligned, or for that major power to guarantee complete protection and support. But just as exclusive alliances of the earlier type have become more difficult to maintain, so alignments become a more necessary form of relationship, even among states of differing political systems. The relationships that are commencing to dominate the international relations of our times are those in which commitments on all sides are conditional, with a premium upon forebearance, concessions, and above all a continuous process of consultation.

Fifth, within the general context sketched above, three basic political alignments in Northeast Asia are apparent: (1) those centering upon the United States, with the U.S.-Japan relation still as close to an alliance as is possible in our times, and with South Korea and Taiwan operating within this orbit, a condition that influences political trends in these two states; (2) the "nonaligned" states—namely, China and North Korea—the former tilting toward Japan and the West in economic and strategic terms while seeking to ward off the political influences that flow from that fact, and the latter strongly within the Leninist orbit, but seeking to avoid being drawn too closely to either the USSR or the PRC; and (3) the alignments centering upon the Soviet Union, in a strict sense limited to Mongolia in this region, but with North Korea available for certain purposes.

IV. The Strategic Configuration Centering Upon Northeast Asia

It is now commonplace to assert that regional and global strategic issues are intertwined, but nowhere is this more evident than with respect to Northeast Asia. To illustrate this fact, and its implications, I shall sketch in broad manner the strategic concerns of the principal states of the region, including subjective fears as well as the calculations that any prudent defense planning requires.

Soviet Strategic Concerns and Policies

The USSR emerged from World War II a badly battered regional power faced with prodigious tasks of reconstruction. Yet in a few years, Moscow presided over a vast empire, controlling all of East Europe and portions of Asia larger in size than those held at the height of czarist power. In addition, it had acquired a new ally of great importance, China. How was this extraordinary advance possible? One reason was that the USSR had been surrounded by weakness—a devastated Europe and Asian societies preoccupied in anticolonial struggles or civil war. Another asset lay in Stalin's diplomatic skills in the wartime period and the Russian determination that supported those skills—a determination to create a multilayered buffer system that would prevent carnage from being visited upon the Soviet people again.

The instinct was defensive, the techniques expansionist. In a very few years, the USSR had managed to take full advantage of its geopolitical position. Together with the new People's Republic of China, it had an opportunity to dominate much of the Eurasian continent. Yet it remained a regional power, with a limited reach beyond the lands adjacent to its borders. In the process of achieving its position, moreover, it had earned the opposition of the one truly global power of that era, the United States. As the Soviets swept over Czechoslovakia and threatened Greece, Washington abandoned its commitment to American-Soviet collaboration and came forth with plans to stop Soviet advances.

Soviet expansion was halted, but in the ensuing years the USSR was able to avoid war and, with enormous sacrifices to its people, devote massive energy and resources to catching up with American strategic power. When Stalin died in 1953, a considerable distance in that direction had been covered. Indeed, a few years later, Russia's Chinese ally,

Mao Zedong, felt that the Soviet Union was sufficiently strong to take risks in confronting the United States on behalf of Beijing and others. Khrushchev was wiser. He knew that the disparity was still substantial. Moreover, without abandoning the drive for strategic "equality," he wanted détente with the United States so that greater attention could be given to the pressing economic and social problems facing his nation. Thirty years later, another Soviet leader would reach a somewhat similar position.

The course of Soviet foreign policy under Khrushchev was erratic. While détente was pursued and caution toward involvement in conflict continued, the Soviet Union took a hard line toward "deviationism" within its empire and succumbed to the temptation to exploit targets of opportunity such as Cuba when they presented themselves. By the end of the Khrushchev era, the alliance with China had been shattered, Eastern Europe was restive notwithstanding the harsh Soviet hand, and relations with the United States were less than satisfactory. In contrast to Khrushchev, Brezhnev was a cautious, conservative, establishment man, a master bureaucrat who built coalitions of existing elites and avoided tampering with the system. It caused him no pain to support the military-industrial complex under which Soviet military power was steadily advanced, with the continuing aim of making the USSR a genuine global power, fully coequal with the United States.

That goal was essentially achieved in the 1970s. A world that had long anticipated bipolarism finally witnessed it. The debate over what constitutes strategic equivalence or other terms applied to military parity will never be completely resolved. Clearly, the answers do not lie wholly in the military realm. The morale and unity of the society at large, its economic foundations and decision-making processes among other considerations, are at least equally important to its weaponry and military personnel in determining its overall power. The issue of quality versus quantity must also be assessed. Many of these factors cannot be accurately measured or even estimated until they are put to the test. Nevertheless, it is a widely held perception—shared by many in the United States and the USSR—that the two nations currently have roughly equal military capacities, including nuclear stockpiles sufficient to level each other many times over in the event of a nuclear war between them.

The recent Soviet emphasis has been upon improving the quality of Soviet weaponry. After a period between 1976 and 1982 when the growth of military expenditures slowed, military spending has again accelerated, presumably in response to the American military buildup that began in the late Carter era. Between one-third and one-fourth of total Soviet military strength is positioned east of the Urals, moreover, representing a dramatic surge of Soviet power in this region since the early 1960s. Of the 192 Soviet divisions, 52 are in Asia, including Central Asia, Siberia and other parts of the Far East, with 40 of these divisions—totaling about 370,000 men—in the Siberian-Far Eastern area. The Pacific Fleet is now the largest of the four Soviet fleets, with about 825 vessels and a total tonnage of 1,700,000, representing nearly one-third of the total strength of the Soviet navy. Approximately one-quarter of the Soviet air force is also in the Far East, including some 300 bombers and 1,600 fighters and fighter-bombers. About one-third of Soviet land-based strategic nuclear forces are east of the Urals, and growing numbers of SS-20 missiles, nuclear-equipped submarines, and aircraft have been deployed into that region.

What is the Soviet perception of threat? The initial major deployments, especially those of ground forces, were in response to China. The growing estrangement between Russia and China involved border hostilities in addition to territorial claims by Beijing's leaders. At the time of greatest tension, at the end of the 1960s, Soviet leaders let it be known that unless Sino-Soviet negotiations on border issues were undertaken, large-scale conflict might break out, and if this occurred, the Soviet Union would not be restricted to conventional weapons. Meanwhile, both conventional forces and nuclear weapons were shifted to the Far East in substantial quantity.

While "the China threat" has greatly subsided, the Soviet forces confronting China have not yet been reduced. On the contrary, partly by intent, partly as a result of responding to other situations, Soviet military encirclement of China is more effective at present than in the 1960s, and more effective than that achieved by any foreign power in history. During the 1950s, when the United States was seeking to contain China, it relied primarily upon naval and air forces operating from Pacific bases. The Soviet Union not only confronts China on the north, west and south with its own sizable military forces or those of allies, but it operates along China's Pacific coastline with a formidable naval fleet.

Tactical adjustments in the disposition of Soviet military forces can and very probably will be made in the interests of furthering Sino-Soviet rapprochement without adversely affecting basic Soviet strategy. But even if this occurs, one thing will not change: an ineradicable Russian suspicion of long-term Chinese intentions. Soviet leaders are convinced that when and if the PRC possesses sufficient military power to sustain bold foreign policies, its leaders will insist that it be accorded recognition as the preeminent nation of Asia, and they will seek to redress old grievances, in the process advancing the Chinese empire—by force, if necessary. The Soviets hope that a coalition of

Asian forces will counter the China threat, and they are prepared to aid such a coalition. Sometimes they have spoken hopefully of an alignment composed of India, Indonesia, and Vietnam—an alignment that seems very remote at present. In any case, the USSR will not reduce its own military guard against the PRC as long as the vision of a resurgent China in the twenty-first century remains vivid.

From a Soviet perspective, however, China is primarily a problem of the future. The problem of the present, as noted, is the advent of a strategic coalition composed of the United States, Japan, and South Korea on Russia's Far Eastern doorstep. Soviet leaders acknowledge that the contributions within this coalition are overwhelmingly American, at least as they affect the USSR, but that does not relieve their anxieties. When Nakasone spoke of Japan being America's aircraft carrier and pledged that, in the event of war, Japan would play its role in seeking to bottle up the Soviet fleet in the Sea of Okhotsk, the Soviets listened. They were also aware that the U.S. nuclear forces in and near South Korea are not necessarily intended for North Korea. Although they publicly depreciate the possibility, moreover, they are still mindful of the once distinct likelihood of Chinese involvement with this coalition. Consequently, they watch with intense interest the low-level strategic ties being forged between the United States and the PRC.

The unfolding of these developments sharpens two concerns of a broader nature that have been deeply implanted in Russian consciousness: the vulnerability of the Soviet Far East and the global encirclement of the USSR by the United States. The Soviet sense of vulnerability in the Far East is understandable. The historic fear of a two-front war served to guide Soviet policies in the early twentieth century, and despite the major strategic changes accompanying the nuclear age, that fear has not disappeared. In the vast, sparsely populated, underdeveloped region of eastern Siberia, the Russians remain largely transients despite strenuous efforts to encourage eastern migration. Transport and communication, moreover, have been massive problems. A second Siberian railway was completed in 1984, but it may take a decade to make it fully operational, and the costs of all undertakings in this region are exceedingly burdensome.

Global encirclement also has its history. When the United States embarked upon its containment policies in the late 1940s, it sought to prevent the USSR from expanding beyond the very considerable region over which it had acquired authority. This was done by a network of alliances enabling the United States to deploy military forces in forward positions, close to the perimeters of the enlarged Soviet empire. It became the Soviet goal to break through or leap over these perimeters, in the process extending its strategic reach globally. While this was accomplished in considerable measure by the end of the 1970s, the absence of an extensive base structure, together with the weak economic and political instruments accompanying Soviet military expansion, continued to concern Russian authorities. The United States was still perceived to be superior in these terms and, as a result, able to project its power more flexibly. Encirclement has remained a reality for Soviet planners, intercontinental ballistic missiles notwithstanding. Thus, in Asia, the quest has been for bases such as in Vietnam to facilitate broader movement. Equipped with its greatly augmented Pacific Fleet, moreover, the USSR seeks new areas of contact such as the South Pacific to give substance to its status as a newly arrived world power.

The U.S. Strategic Debate and Current Policies

It remains for Mikhail Gorbachev or his successors to find means of adding influence to power in a world accustomed to regarding the USSR as inferior to the advanced industrial societies in almost all respects other than military. Meanwhile, the United States is forced to ponder its own strategic priorities and policies in a rapidly changing international environment. Shortly after the close of World War II, the United States established commitments that have remained intact for forty years. Its first attention was given to Western Europe, a region deemed vital to the preservation of any political and economic order that would accord with American interests. At an early point, however, it was realized that East Asia would play a steadily greater role in determining the global balance, economically and politically as well as militarily. In the years that followed, although the United States was drawn into other regions by events, and the commitment to the Middle East in particular took on a life of its own for various reasons, Western Europe and East Asia have remained at the center of U.S. strategic concerns.

The task of containment is always more complex than that of expansion. Those who would contain can rarely pick the ideal battleground. They must often decide about marginal cases -what the costs of making a commitment are, and what also are the future costs if a commitment is not made. A shrewd Chinese statesman, Zhou Enlai, once suggested a strategy to employ against the United States. Release many fleas (guerrilla movements, insurrections, etc.), he suggested, and while the United States is trying to keep its fingers on some fleas, others will escape. In a sense, that was Communist strategy in the 1950s when the USSR and the PRC were united, with their military weakness compensated in some measure by the ideological and nationalistic ferment throughout the non-Western world.

Although it was easy for American policy-makers to agree that the Pacific-Asian theater was of vital consequence to American interests, it was far more difficult to reach a consensus upon the appropriate U.S. strategy for this region. The initial debate transpired between those who advocated an island *cordon sanitaire* approach versus those who believed that it was essential to preserve certain enclaves on the Asian continent against communist control. The former strategy envisaged the containment of Soviet-Chinese power by reliance upon American air and sea power, utilizing the chain of islands stretching from Japan to the Philippines. Adherents of this strategy strongly opposed pitting American soldiers against the limitless manpower of Asia. But others doubted that if the Asian continent were completely controlled by a Moscow-Beijing axis, the offshore island states could survive, given the adverse economic and political as well as military repercussions that would ensue.

This unresolved dispute made its contribution to the two Asian wars in which the United States was subsequently involved. The signals emanating from Washington, both before the Korean war and before the U.S. military involvement in Vietnam, were of adherence to the island *cordon sanitaire* strategy. The North Koreans thus attacked South Korea, believing that an American response was unlikely. And in Vietnam, the North made its plans after 1954, never realizing that in a decade, a massive American military commitment would begin.

The Guam Declaration of 1969 stipulated a compromise, deliberately vague in certain implications. American allies, whether island states or continental states, would be expected to play the primary role in their own defense, but if attacked, the United States would provide assistance, with reliance principally on air and sea power. This doctrine—of critical importance to states like South Korea and Thailand—has not yet been tested. Meanwhile, the political context in which strategies were earlier debated has changed dramatically. Between 1949 and 1969, the PRC was regarded as a threat to America's Asian allies, and hence to the United States itself, not without reason. Since that time, China has ceased to be such a threat, and there is no indication that this situation will change in the foreseeable future.

Old issues were thus replaced by new ones in the course of U.S.-PRC normalization, as indicated earlier. The central strategic issue pertaining to the Pacific-Asian region debated within the Carter administration was whether a policy of equidistance between the USSR and the PRC should be pursued or the effort should be made to build a strategic alignment with the PRC against the USSR. As noted, this issue was determined in the end not by American leaders but by the Chinese. Nevertheless, as long as relations with the USSR are minimal and strongly hostile, the cultivation of a low-level strategic relationship with the PRC will have an appeal in Washington.

Recent American strategy in the Pacific-Asian region has been an integral part of U.S. global strategy. It has rested upon MAD (Mutual Assured Destruction), the maintenance of the existing network of bases enabling forward deployment, and an increased premium upon mobility together with ever more sophisticated weaponry. The United States cannot expect to match the USSR's military strength in East Asia quantitatively. When the Reagan administration's plan for a 600-ship navy is realized in a few years, additional Trident-class nuclear-powered submarines, new cruisers, and aircraft carriers together with refitted battleships will join existing ships to constitute the core of the 7th Fleet. Currently, that fleet has less than 50 combat ships and auxiliaries, with slightly over 40,000 naval personnel. The 3d Fleet, with over 150 ships and auxilaries, is based in the eastern Pacific, protecting the continental United States and Hawaii but available farther to the west in case of need. The Pacific Air Force consists of approximately 500 bombers and fighters, manned by 37,500 personnel, and with auxiliaries available from the Military Airlift Command and other sources as required. Ground forces in the theater are strictly limited, numbering only slightly under 40,000, almost all in South Korea. An additional 26,000 marines are stationed in Okinawa, with a small contingent in the Philippines.

Since U.S. strategy is centrally geared to its global power, and specifically its nuclear capacity, it must depend much more heavily upon the conventional capacities of its allies than is required of the USSR. Hence, the United States must be deeply concerned about the political and economic health of those states with which it is aligned. Instability within key Asian states may well constitute the gravest threat to security within the region, and weaknesses here cannot be remedied by military means alone.

Recent trends have created additional challenges to the doctrine of Mutual Assured Destruction upon which the basic strategies of both the United States and the USSR rest, further complicating the future. The threat of "nuclear winter," valid or not, raises profound questions about the use of nuclear weapons and could cause additional erosion of the credibility of the U.S. commitments in Europe and Asia. Yet while the possibilities of large-scale conventional war are being upgraded in some analyses, the political disadvantages under which the United States labors in placing renewed emphasis on conventional preparedness are serious. The Reagan administration has chosen to launch the United States upon another route, that of Strategic Defense Initiative (SDI). Whether this route is feasible and, beyond that, whether it is stabilizing or destabilizing remain hotly debated questions.

Whatever the facts, it is a widespread assumption in Asia that the two superpowers have achieved a rough strategic equivalence both in the Pacific-Asian region and globally. Hence, it is presumed that neither will take the risk of attacking the other, and that sooner or later a new strategic arms limitation agreement will be achieved, despite the disappointing Reykjavik meetings. It is now clear, moreover, that Asia's security concerns must and will be a part of any global agreement. Meanwhile, virtually every Asian state, whatever its own defense policies, is inclined to regard the USSR as essentially an American problem.

Trends in Japanese Strategic Policies

Epitomizing this view is Japan—or, more accurately, a majority of the Japanese public and politicians. There is no question that Japanese in sizable and growing numbers have regarded the Soviet Union as a hostile country, and a threat in general terms. They do not believe, however, that the USSR will attack Japan except in the context of a general war. Given the strong allergy to nuclear weapons and the past comfort of being encased in the American cocoon, most Japanese are loath to shed their minimal-risk defense policies to assume a regional security role, or even to achieve adequate defense capabilities with respect to their own territory. Experts assert that with its current capacities, Japan could not defend itself against invasion for more than a few days. They testify that the current level of defense expenditures will not permit Japan to meet existing commitments for regional surveillance in the near future. Yet only a few Japanese seem troubled by these facts. The Nakasone administration or its successor may creep past the one percent barrier governing military expenditures, but this act—when it comes—will not be a political asset at home.

One should not overlook the steps that have been taken. As is often noted, Japan now has the eighth largest military establishment in the world (although most of those that are larger are Japan's neighbors). There can be little question that while the Japanese forces are limited and geared solely to defense, they are highly modern in conventional terms. Japanese military technology, indeed, is of interest to the United States, and under special agreement it is to be made available. Moreover, joint defense planning and exercises between Japan and the United States have been routinized and are working well. In addition, as indicated, Japan has established loose connections with the defense establishments of both South Korea and the PRC as well as those of Taiwan, exchanging information. In principle, Japan is committed to conducting air surveillance in the region up to 200 miles and sea surveillance up to 1,000 miles to the east and south. Beyond this, agreements exist between the United States and Japan with respect to the defense of South Korea should it be attacked, and the presence of U.S. F-16s on Hokkaido are concrete evidence of Japan's role in the containment of the USSR.

Nevertheless, charges of Japanese militarism are wild exaggerations, and the vision of an Asian NATO centering upon the United States, Japan and the ROK will remain a dream—good or bad depending upon the dreamer—for the foreseeable future. As suggested earlier, Japan will opt for neither pacifism nor Gaullism but build incrementally on a strategy already sketched out, counting heavily upon the United States and, beyond this, a world where good fortune greatly outweighs disaster in the years ahead.

China's Strategic Perspectives

China's strategic perceptions have already been indicated in broad outline. Most PRC leaders believe that the Soviet Union will constitute a long-term problem, although there is reason to believe that some differences of opinion on this matter exist within current Chinese elites. Even those who view the USSR as a threat, however, see the Russians primarily as a force constraining Chinese options and possibly complicating Chinese politics rather than as a potential invader. Thus, the problem can be handled over time. No urgency exists. The policies and status of the United States, the other superpower, evoke mixed feelings. Its renewed strength globally and in Asia permits the PRC to pursue nonalignment with a more relaxed attitude. Further, the United States does not now pose a security threat, nor is it likely to do so in the future. On the other hand, American policies toward various parts of the Third World are viewed as doomed to failure and likely to cause heightened tension. The unwillingness of the two superpowers to find a path to strategic arms limitations is also acclaimed to be dangerous. And China regards SDI as a threat to its own nuclear deterrent.

The PRC will continue to rely upon a limited nuclear deterrent together with a large, gradually modernized conventional force. It may be exploring the benefits of a tactical nuclear capacity. Reversing an earlier position, PRC leaders no longer take a relaxed attitude toward nuclear proliferation. Although Beijing's main preoccupation is with economic growth, it is not ignoring the fourth modernization, that of the military. The weeding out of old senior officers and the force reduction by some 25 percent is a necessary first step in that process. To obtain modern technology, even of a limited and "defensive" type, as is being acquired from the United States, is a second step. For several decades, however, China's primary defense will rest

64

with its sheer bulk. When the Soviet Union was earlier contemplating military alternatives, it must have realized that even a limited strike or the seizure of some portion of Chinese territory could provoke unending warfare. Afghanistan has surely made that fact more graphic.

If China is reasonably secure from external attack, do the small countries on the peripheries of this colossus need to fear the PRC several decades hence, and could China be a threat even to the USSR at some point in the next century? These issues have already been raised in a different context. While there is no clear answer, two factors are less than comforting. First, the combination of historic precedent and the current nationalist tides suggests that within China, there is a strong urge for the reassertion of Chinese greatness. Even in the Communist era, Chinese leaders have periodically reverted to tradition in handling small "barbarians" on their borders, rewarding good ones, punishing bad ones.

China, moreover, remains a nation dissatisfied with the status quo, both with respect to certain territorial dispositions and with respect to the prestige accorded it. Granting these two facts, however, a repetition of the past course is by no means inevitable. The Asia of the twenty-first century will not be the Asia of the past. Nor can China act with impunity against the interests of the world's other major states. In particular, the USSR will make certain that its military strength is sufficient to deter China from expansion in areas vital to it.

What generalizations can be drawn from the strategic policies and relations of the major powers, as they apply to Northeast Asia?

First, despite some zones of tension, notably the divided states, East Asia is unlikely to be the seedbed of a global war. Taking into account all of the factors—political and economic as well as strategic—each of the major states, and most importantly the United States and the USSR, have a mix of strengths and weaknesses that preclude great risk-taking. Neither superpower, moreover, is profoundly dissatisfied with the territorial status quo in this region.

Yet it is equally important to assert that if a major Soviet-American conflict breaks out elsewhere, East Asia will surely be involved unless that conflict can be promptly contained. This region, and especially Northeast Asia, is far too important in every respect to escape in the event of an intercontinental war.

Second, the simple balance of weaponry—conventional and nuclear—favors the USSR in the Northeast Asia theater, but when the full range of factors constituting what the Japanese have labeled "comprehensive security" is taken into account, the Russians have reason to be less than satisfied with their position. Strategically and politically, they stand virtually alone, whereas the United States has a network of meaningful ties with the most important Northeast Asian states. The task confronting the USSR can be easily defined. It must find ways to build economic and political components into its Asian policies. Otherwise, it will continue to be regarded as the most militarist of all the major powers in the region, to its detriment. It is this patently obvious fact that underlies the new Soviet Asian initiatives.

Third, while security ties of a regional nature have grown in Northeast Asia, centering upon the U.S. - Japan relationship and extending to South Korea, with strands also reaching China and Taiwan, a regional security structure is not remotely possible at this point or in the near future. Thus, the burdens upon the United States will be disproportionately heavy, and this may cause further strain.

Fourth, future alterations in strategic policies on the part of the major states are very likely in an era when the risks attendant to nuclear conflict continue to rise, when the difficulty of winning small conventional wars is repeatedly demonstrated, and when terrorism has increasing advantages when employed against a more powerful foe—being the cheapest, least risky means of seeking to effect change.

Fifth, despite the importance of a broad strategic equilibrium, security for most Northeast Asian states will be increasingly related to their internal economic and political health. In the future as in the past, domestic upheaval is the surest route to external intervention.

V. Reflections on U.S. Policy in Asia

Are there lessons for U.S. policy toward Asia in the foregoing analysis? In my opinion, the following prescriptions are valid, although there must be no illusion that the United States alone can reduce tensions where they exist, resolve all ongoing problems, or strengthen the causes of regional security and development.

First, the greatest obligation on the part of the United States is to put its own economic house in order. The American economy must be better managed than has been the case in recent decades. Reforms or a reorientation of thinking has begun, but barely. We must bring the massive yearly budgetary deficits under control, both by increasing taxes and by reducing governmental spending. The recent shocking revelations of waste and corruption in defense and space programs suggest that in some of our most critical—and most expensive—programs, much could be done better at lower cost. This must receive the full attention of the White House and the Congress.

It is also essential for American enterprises to rethink their corporate strategies and mode of operations. Immediate profits need not be the all-consuming goal at the expense of market share. Research and development demand the fullest attention, but beyond this, it should not be beneath American entrepreneurs to develop marketable products for cultures other than our own. The restoration of American competitiveness, it is now widely recognized, is vital to our health and that of others. This will require the cooperation of management and labor. It also involves an appropriate mix of effective government policies and private sector initiatives.

Second, we must make a sustained effort to reach an agreement with the Russians on strategic arms limitation based upon mutual, verifiable reductions that turn us away from further escalation of the arms race. In the period immediately ahead, Americans and Russians hold their own survival and that of others very largely in their hands. There is a basis for compromise on the critical issues including SDI where a dividing line can be drawn between research, on the one hand, and testing and deployment, on the other. The moment must be seized. It is now.

Third, we have every right to expect the nations aligned with the United States to do more on behalf of themselves and on behalf of the region they inhabit, not merely with respect to security but also in economic and political terms. A wealthy nation like Japan must assume greater responsibilities for regional and international security and development. So-called developing nations must adopt rational economic and political policies that serve the needs of their own people. Such policies can be and, for the most part, have been discerned. Now political leaders must implement them. In broad terms, it is entirely appropriate for the United States to apply "quid pro quo" policies more rigorously, to say in effect, "if you do this, we will do that; otherwise, we cannot make the same commitment."

Fourth, in the coming age of alignments rather than alliances, the United States should foster a range of private instruments of discussion and consultation to augment the public bodies that exist. We need more contact with the diverse groups that make up the pluralist societies with which we have close relations. Official bodies alone do not suffice.

Fifth, East Asia is ready for a series of loose Pacific-Asian forums, economic and social in nature. The basis for a tight, formal regional structure does not now exist, and it is not likely to come into being soon. But the probing toward regional consultation now under way as well as the existence of global and regional bodies dedicated to specific purposes are logical concomitants of our growing interdependence.

Finally, with reference to some of the specific issues that confront the United States in Northeast Asia, the following steps should be undertaken:

A private U.S.-Japan council should be created with appropriate subgroups to explore medium- to long-range issues in the relations between our two countries. Such a body would report to the two governments and have a permanent existence, with members drawn from the key sectors of the society and having a tenure sufficient to ensure conversance with the issues and continuity of policy.

Political evolution in South Korea must be supported, with a policy that walks the difficult path between indifference and heavy intervention on issues of human rights, relying principally upon keeping contact with a diversity of groups, urging democratic procedures upon all elements, and supporting a range of dialogues between Americans and Koreans in the private sector.

On the economic front, Korean policies along with those of the other NICs and of China must be integrated with U.S. capacities and needs to ensure that the history of U.S.-Japan economic relations in recent times is not repeated. This will require multilateral as well as bilateral efforts.

There is no reason to move toward the recognition of North Korea at this time, in either de jure or de facto terms. Pyongyang has yet to prove that it is prepared to deal with other nations, including South Korea, in accordance with an internationally sanctioned code of behavior. Informal contacts of an academic or similar nature, however, may provide a basis for future interaction if and when North Korean policies change.

It is in the U.S. national interest to see China achieve economic growth and political stability, and a wide range of supportive policies to these ends is appropriate. Great caution, however, is warranted in assisting China with military modernization, taking full account of the sensitivities of other Asians and the uncertainties surrounding the political-strategic future of China itself.

No need exists to alter the current relations between the United States and Taiwan, but the principles suggested with respect to South Korea apply.

Conditions warrant renewed efforts on the part of the United States to open cultural and diplomatic ties with the People's Republic of Mongolia.

One final comment seems in order. If the problems confronting East Asia and the major powers so intimately involved in the region seem formidable, the opportunities for pioneering ventures in economic, political and strategic cooperation are also extensive. The human and natural resources of the Pacific-Asian area make it the logical pacesetter of the century ahead. And with its future, the future of the United States is inextricably connected. Our priorities and our policies must reflect that fact.

Suggested Reading

Barnett, A. Doak and Ralph N. Clough, eds., *Modernizing China: Post-Mao Reform and Development*, Boulder, CO: Westview Press, 1986.

Johnson, U. Alexis, George R. Packard and Alfred D. Wilhelm, Jr., eds., *China Policy for the Next Decade: The Atlantic Council's Committee on China Policy*, Cambridge, MA: Oelgeschlager, Gunn & Hain, 1984.

Lincoln, Edward J., *Japan's Economic Role in Northeast Asia*, New York: The Asia Society, and Lanham, MD: University Press of America, 1986.

Pye, Lucien W. and Mary W. Pye, *Asian Power and Politics: The Cultural Dimensions of Authority*, Cambridge, MA: Belknap Press of Harvard Press, 1985.

Scalapino, Robert A., Seizaburo Sato and Jusuf Wanandi, eds., *Asian Economic Development-Present and Future*, Berkeley, CA: University of California at Berkeley, Institute of East Asian Studies, 1985.

Scalapino, Robert A., Seizaburo Sato and Jusuf Wanandi, eds., *Asian Political Institutionalization*, Berkeley, CA: University of California at Berkeley, Institute of East Asian Studies, 1986.

Scalapino, Robert A., Seizaburo Sato and Jusuf Wanandi, eds., *Internal and External Security Issues in Asia*, Berkeley, CA: University of California at Berkeley, Institute of East Asian Studies, 1986.

Solomon, Richard H. and Masataka Kosaka, eds., *The Soviet-Far East Military Buildup: Nuclear Dilemma and Asian Security*, Dover, MA: Auburn House Publishing Company, 1986.

Zagoria, Donald S., *Soviet Policy in East Asia*, New Haven, CT: Yale University Press, 1982.

About the Author

Robert A. Scalapino is Robson Research Professor of Government and Director of the Institute of East Asian Studies at the University of California at Berkeley. He is also editor of *Asian Survey*, a scholarly monthly journal. His recent books include *Modern China and Its Revolutionary Process* (with George T. Yu), *Asia and the Road Ahead*, and *The Foreign Policy of Modern Japan*.

ᴙ D